CHANNEL ZERO
JENNIE ONE

BY
(writer) **BRIAN WOOD**
BECKY CLOONAN (artist)

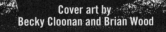

Cover art by
Becky Cloonan and Brian Wood

interior photo and book design by Brian Wood

www.brianwood.com
www.estrigious.com/becky
www.ait-planetlar.com

AiT/PLANET LAR
SAN FRANCISCO

Channel Zero: JENNIE ONE by Brian Wood and Becky Cloonan

Published by AiT/Planet Lar, 2034 47th Avenue, San Francisco, CA 94116

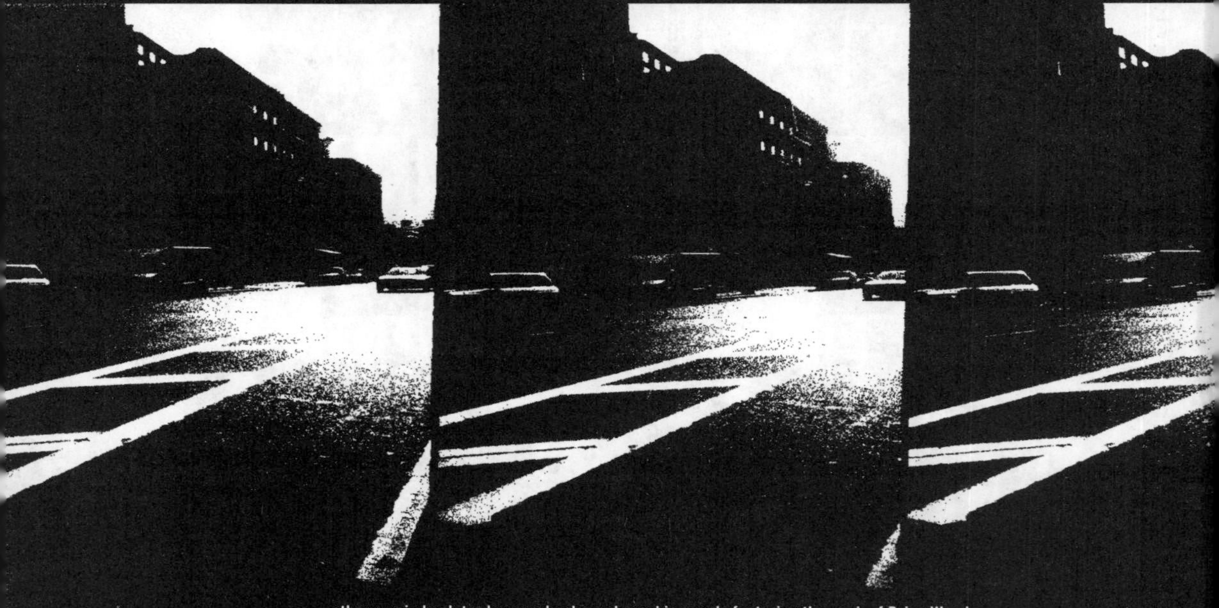

other comic book trade paperbacks and graphic novels featuring the work of Brian Wood
available from AiT/Planet Lar

CHANNEL ZERO
by Brian Wood

PUBLIC DOMAIN: A Channel Zero designbook
by Brian Wood

COUSCOUS EXPRESS
by Brian Wood and Brett Weldele

THE COURIERS
by Brian Wood and Rob G

Second edition January 2004
First edition January 2003

10 9 8 7 6 5 4 3 2

Cover illustration and design by Brian Wood and Becky Cloonan
ISBN: 1-932051-07-4

JENNIE ONE

I remember backpacking into the city in 1991, a hick skater punk rock kid from Northern Vermont, looking for something to happen to me, something exciting, creative, dangerous, sexy. I enrolled in art school, got a job bike messengering, and soaked in the culture. NYC in the mid-nineties was a sick place, an uneasy, plastic-coated Rudy Giuliani-flavored playground with the riot cops peeking at you from just around the corner. Rents soared, the police brutalized innocent people, artists were persecuted, small business squeezed out, replaced with superstores and theme restaurants. And in the middle of this quiet horror and suppressed chaos, I created CHANNEL ZERO and told it all to fuck off, hizzoner included. That was in 1997.

Then in 2002, we entered a whole new period of social freakshow, violent repression and political corruption. Right around that time I met artist Becky Cloonan, who was just as pissed off and hungry as I was a decade earlier. I sat down and wrote JENNIE ONE for her to draw.

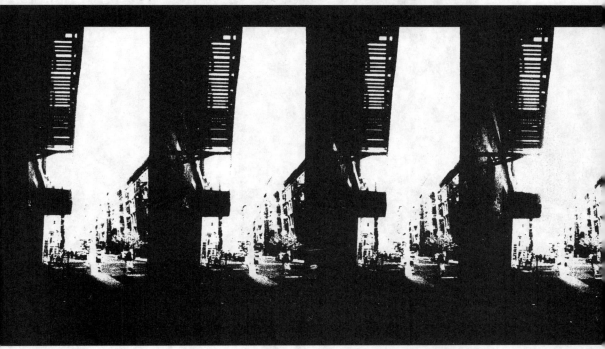

I'm almost 31 as I write this now, nearing the end of my punk rock New York City art terrorist days. Becky's turned 21, and is just getting started on hers. I gave her something she would want to draw, something she could relate to, events she's lived. Something for the shared histories and experiences we've both had. JENNIE ONE is custom-built for her talents and sensibilities. Check it out. It shows. No one could have done this better than her.

-Brian Wood, Brooklyn, 2003

NEW YORK CITY.

NOW.

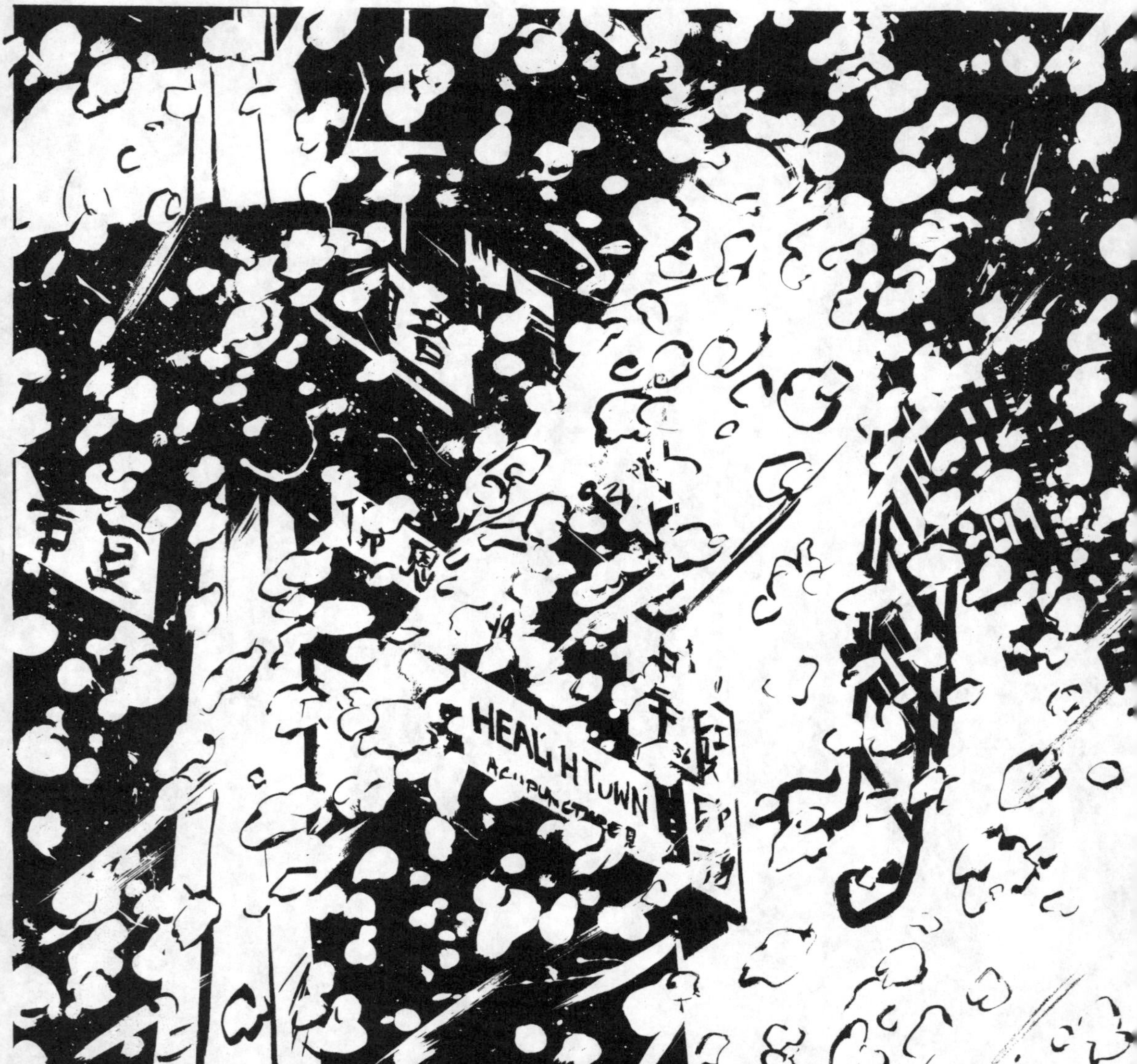

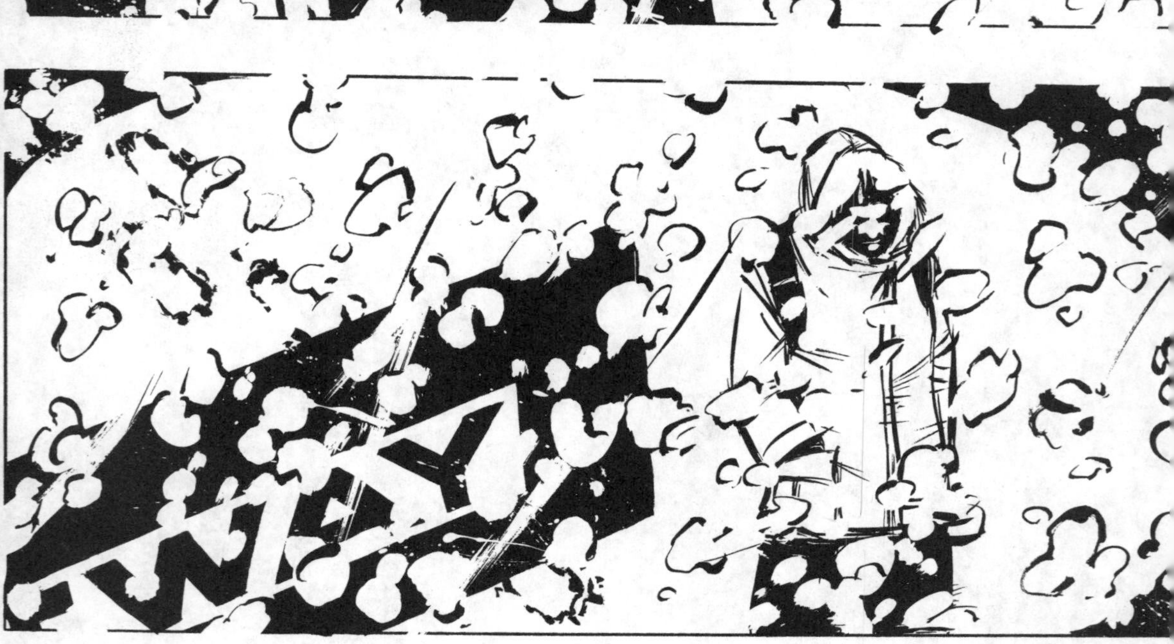

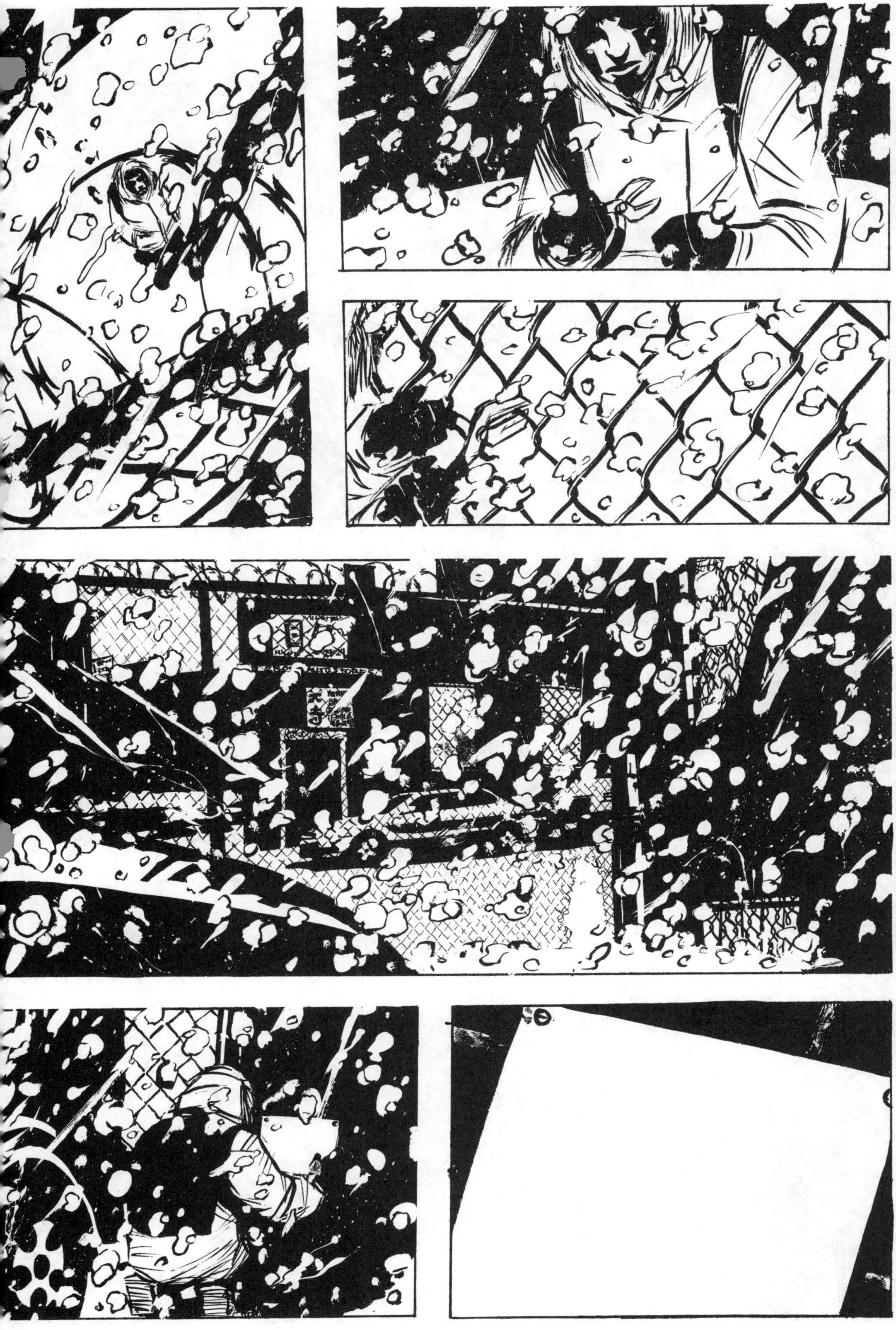

I REMEMBER THIS DAY.

THE MOTT ST. RIOTS

JULY—AUGUST
THE SUMMER OF THE CLEAN ACT
IN MEMORY OF OUR FALLEN

ROSS GULLEY
MELISSA DEJESUS
JOHNATHAN MUKAI
VERONICA CASSON
ROBERTO FLORES
JOHN GRINER
LUIS W. REYES
NIKHOLAS GAZIN
FRANKIE PANNONE
RYAN SOLSKI
YANG FAN
CIPRIANO

GAMAL HENNESSY
KHOEUN TEP
JAMES GRIFFIN
SHAKIR TURTON
JOHN AMBROSE
SALVATORE INGA
VANESSA SATONE
JENNIFER QUICK
MATTHEW WOODSON
HWAN SUK CHA
PAULA VAN
DEREK BEAR
RYLAN PERRY
ELLIOTT STURGEON

ALANA ROBERTS
BEN GERALD
MIN KWON
STEVE UY
HANSEL PEREZ
JAUN'E KIM
MAYUMI KOB
LIZ BAILLIE
LARRY CHY
CHRIS MCD
AMY KIM
MING F
MARCO
PEDRO

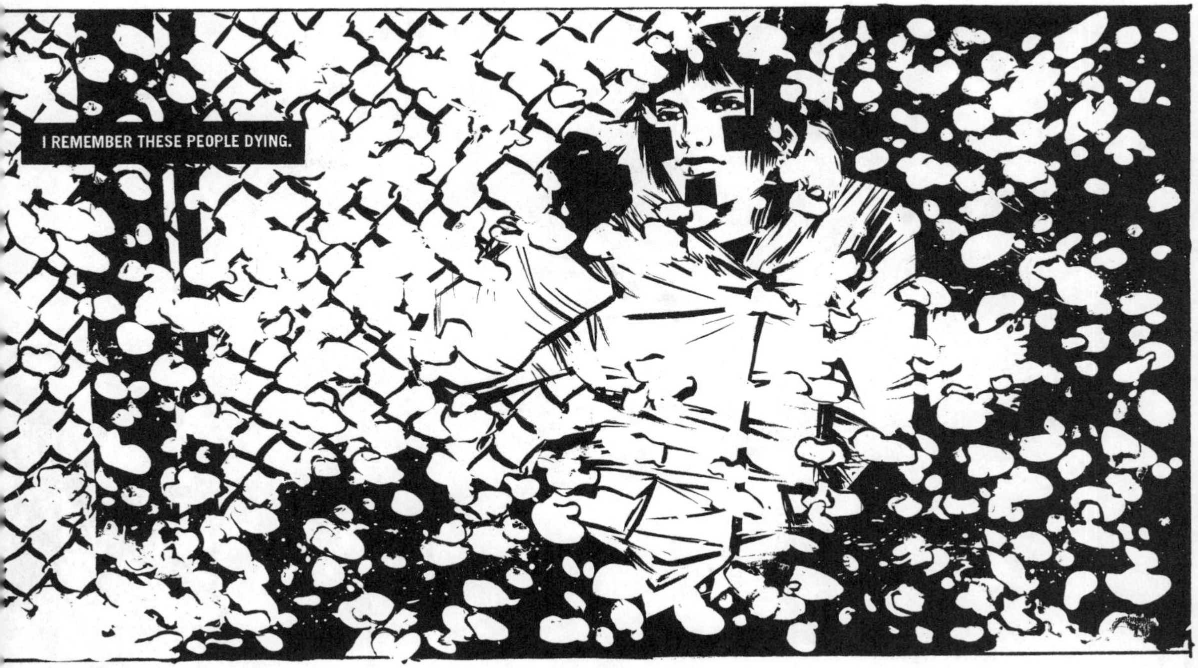
I REMEMBER THESE PEOPLE DYING.

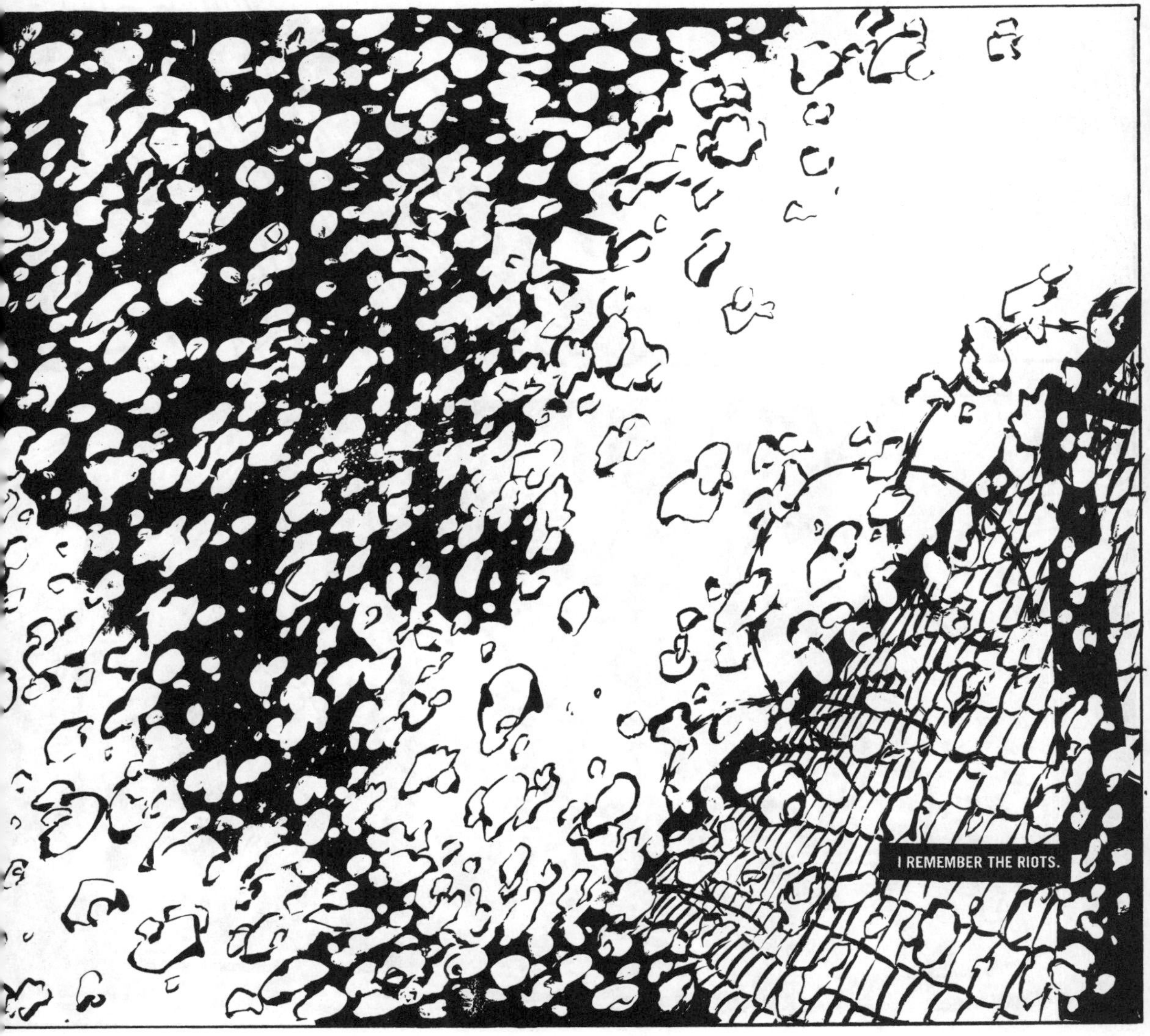
I REMEMBER THE RIOTS.

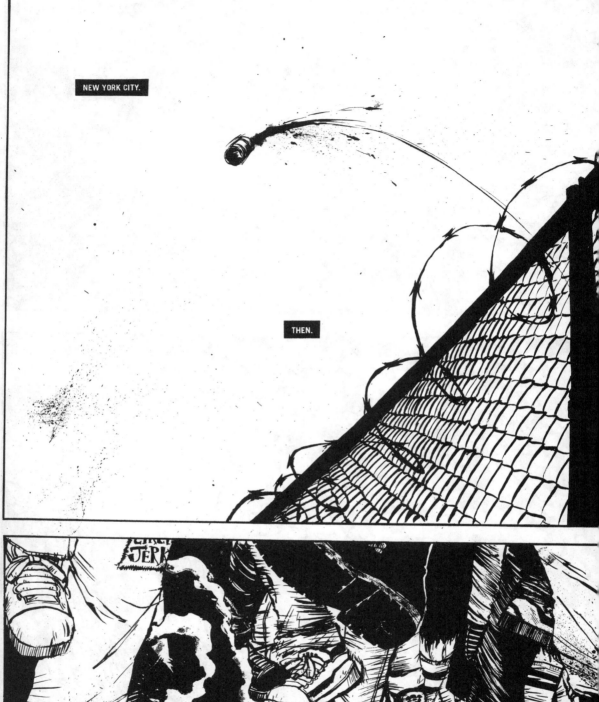

NEW YORK CITY.

THEN.

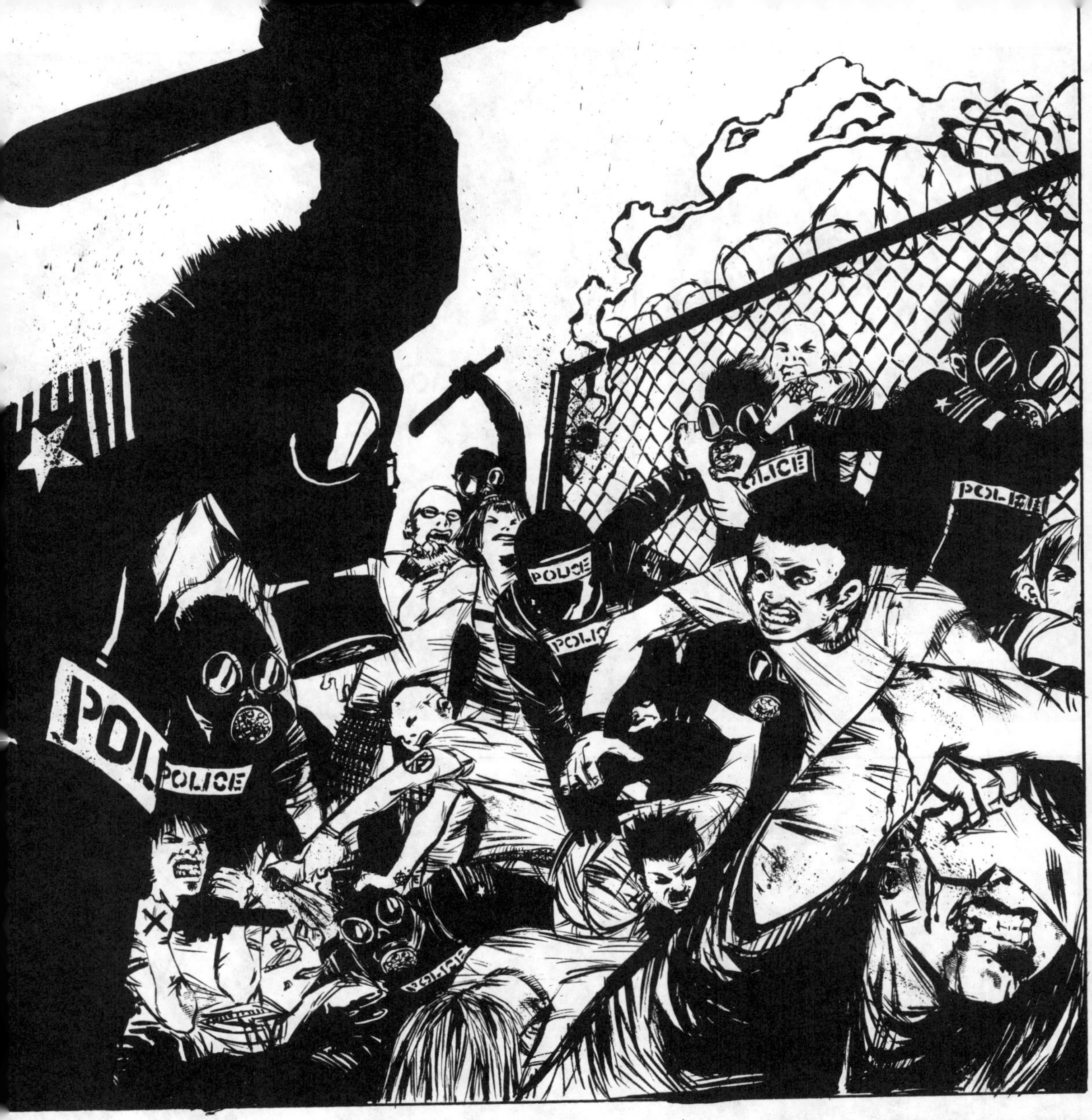
POLICE
POLICE
POLICE

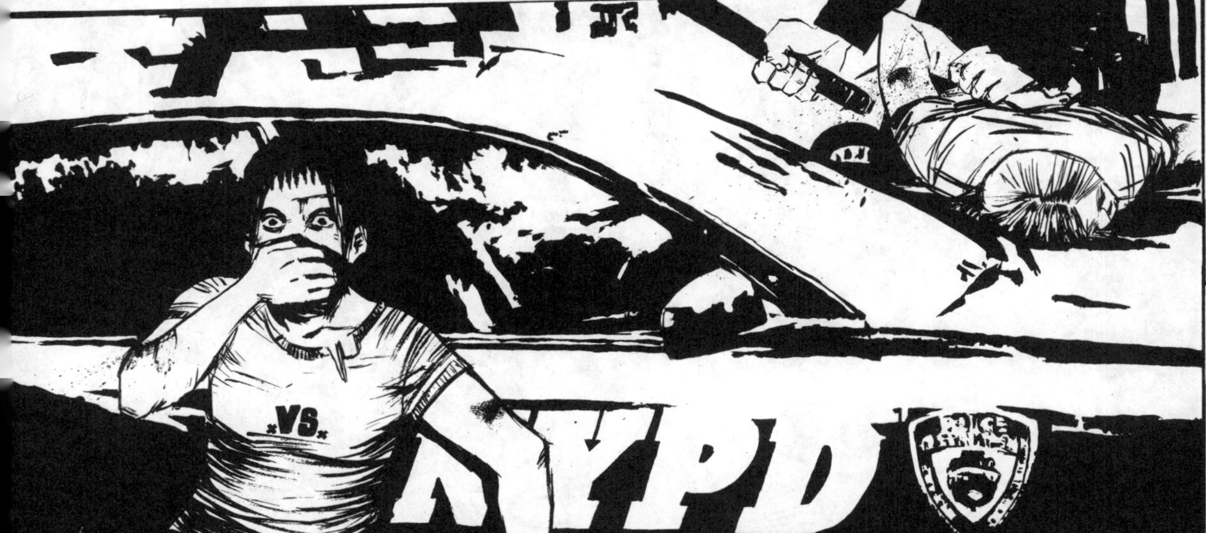
VS.
NYPD

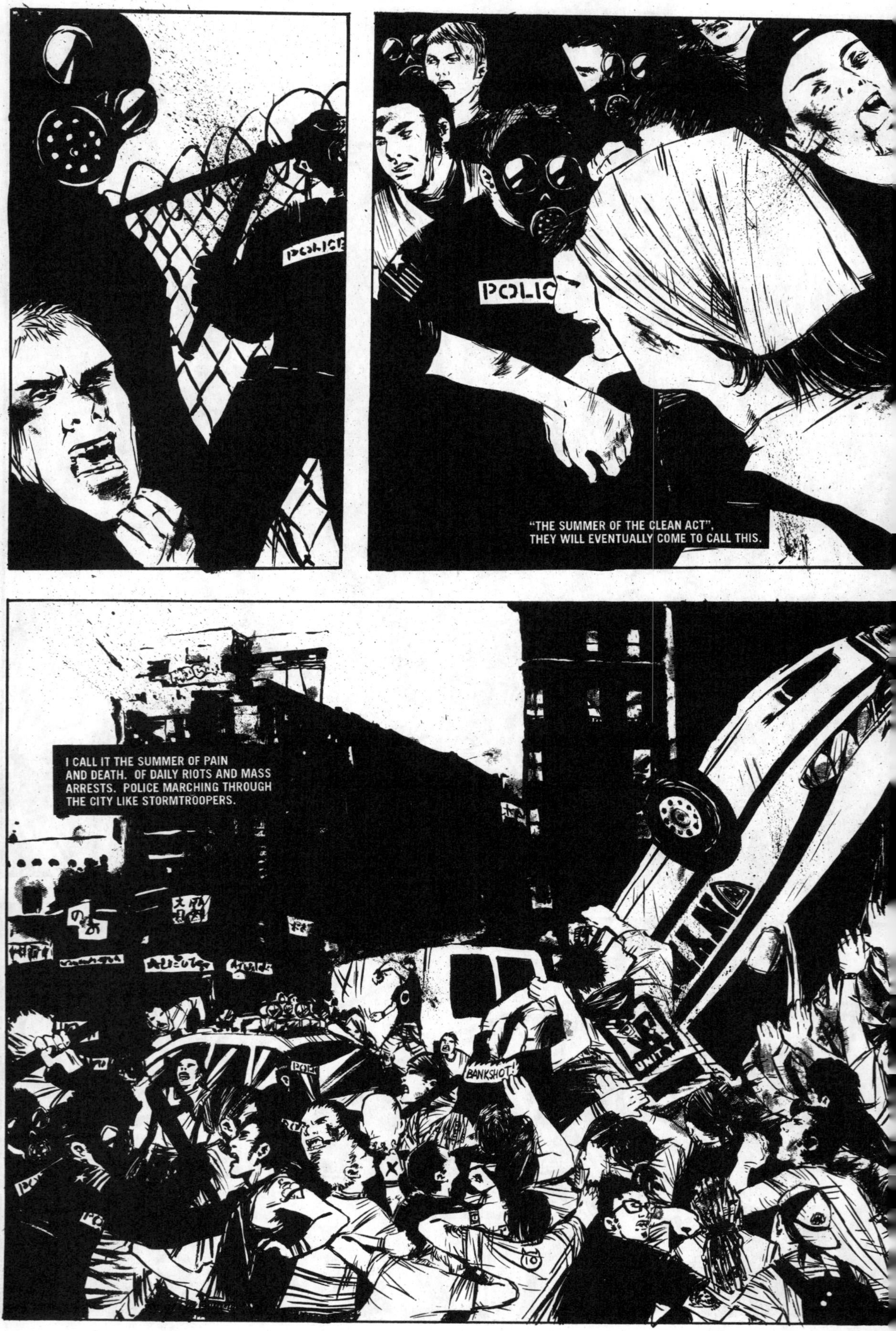
POLICE
POLIC
"THE SUMMER OF THE CLEAN ACT", THEY WILL EVENTUALLY COME TO CALL THIS.
I CALL IT THE SUMMER OF PAIN AND DEATH. OF DAILY RIOTS AND MASS ARRESTS. POLICE MARCHING THROUGH THE CITY LIKE STORMTROOPERS.
BANKSHOT!
UNITY

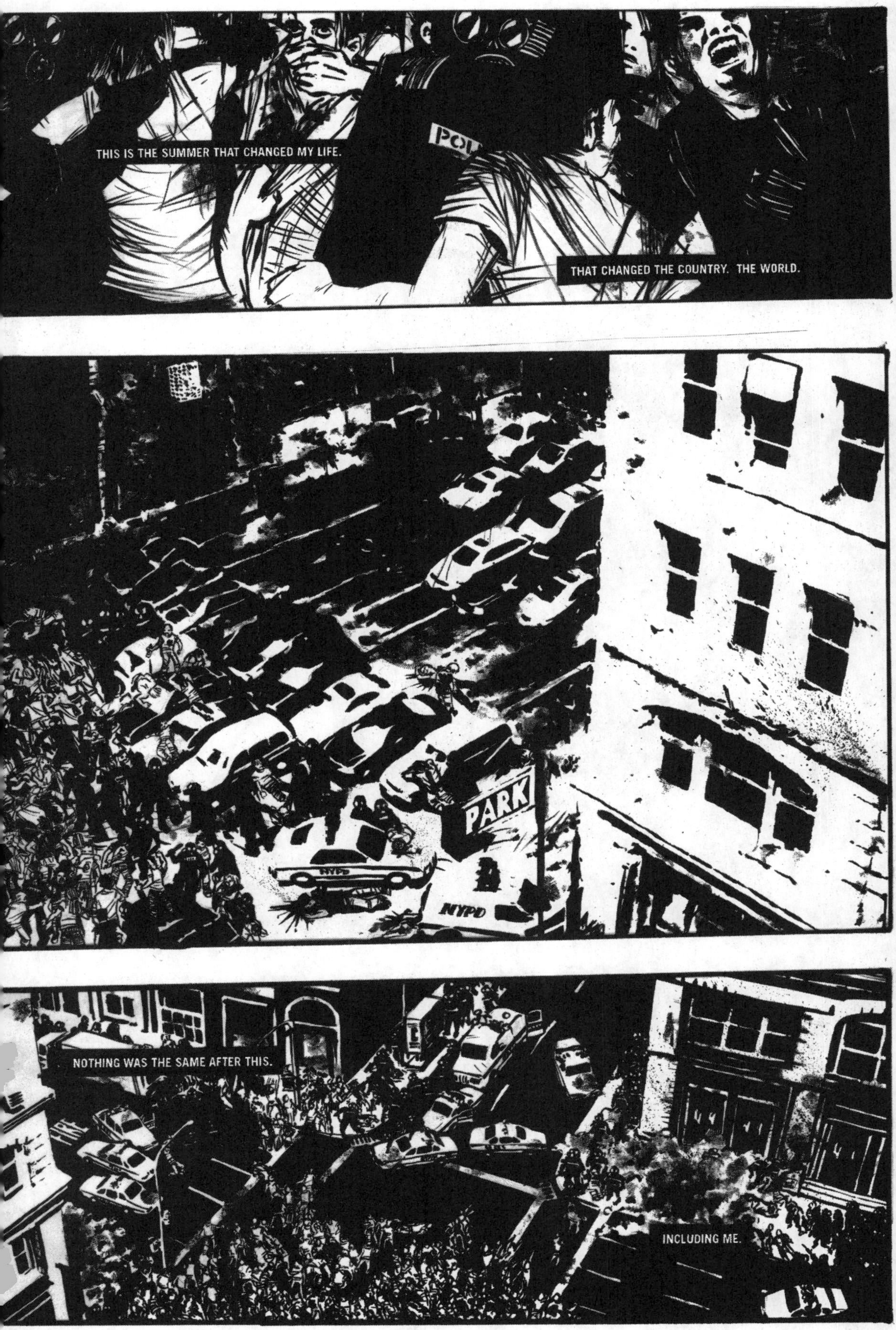
THIS IS THE SUMMER THAT CHANGED MY LIFE.
THAT CHANGED THE COUNTRY. THE WORLD.
PARK
NYPD
NYPD
NOTHING WAS THE SAME AFTER THIS.
INCLUDING ME.

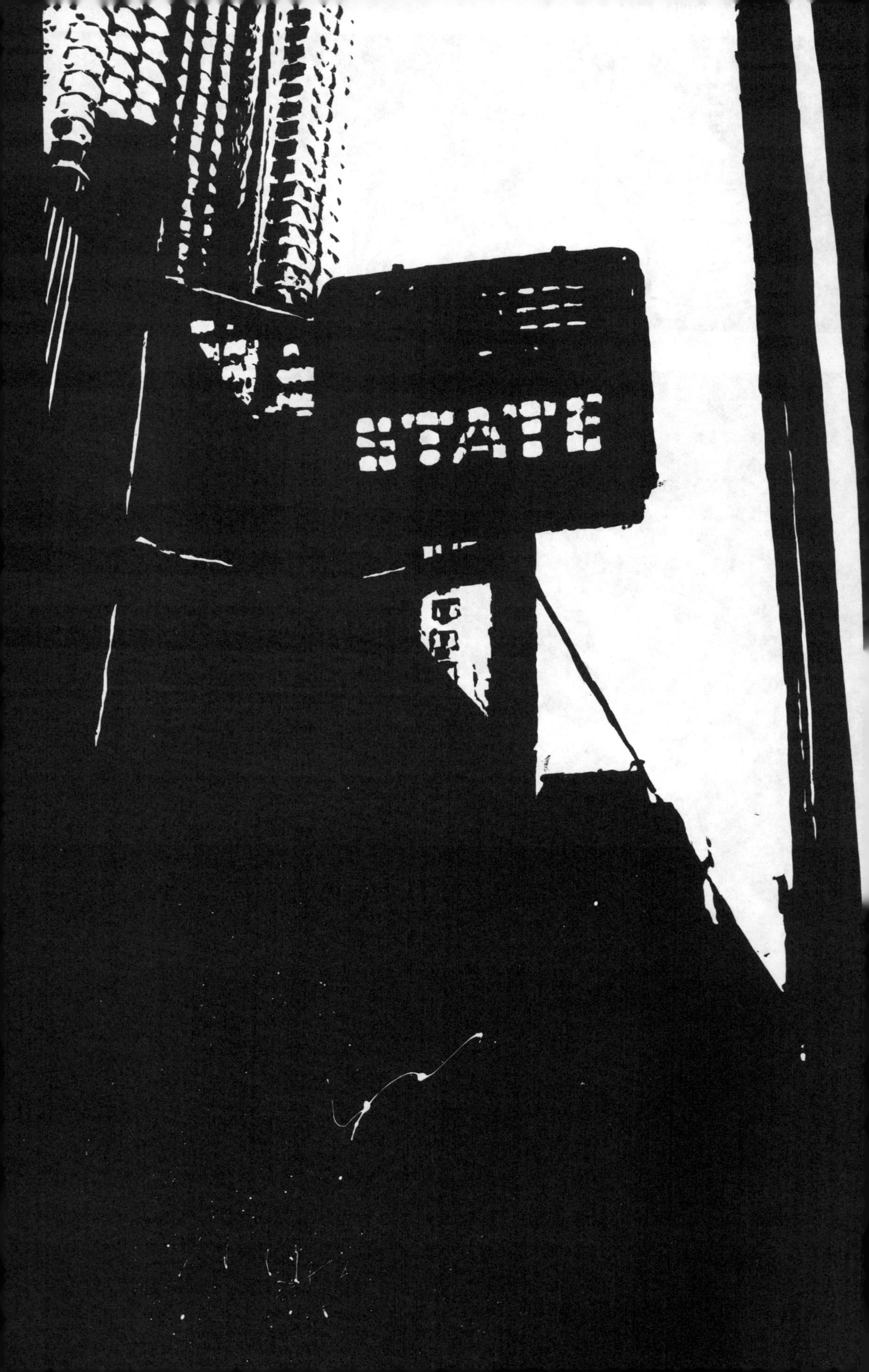
STATE

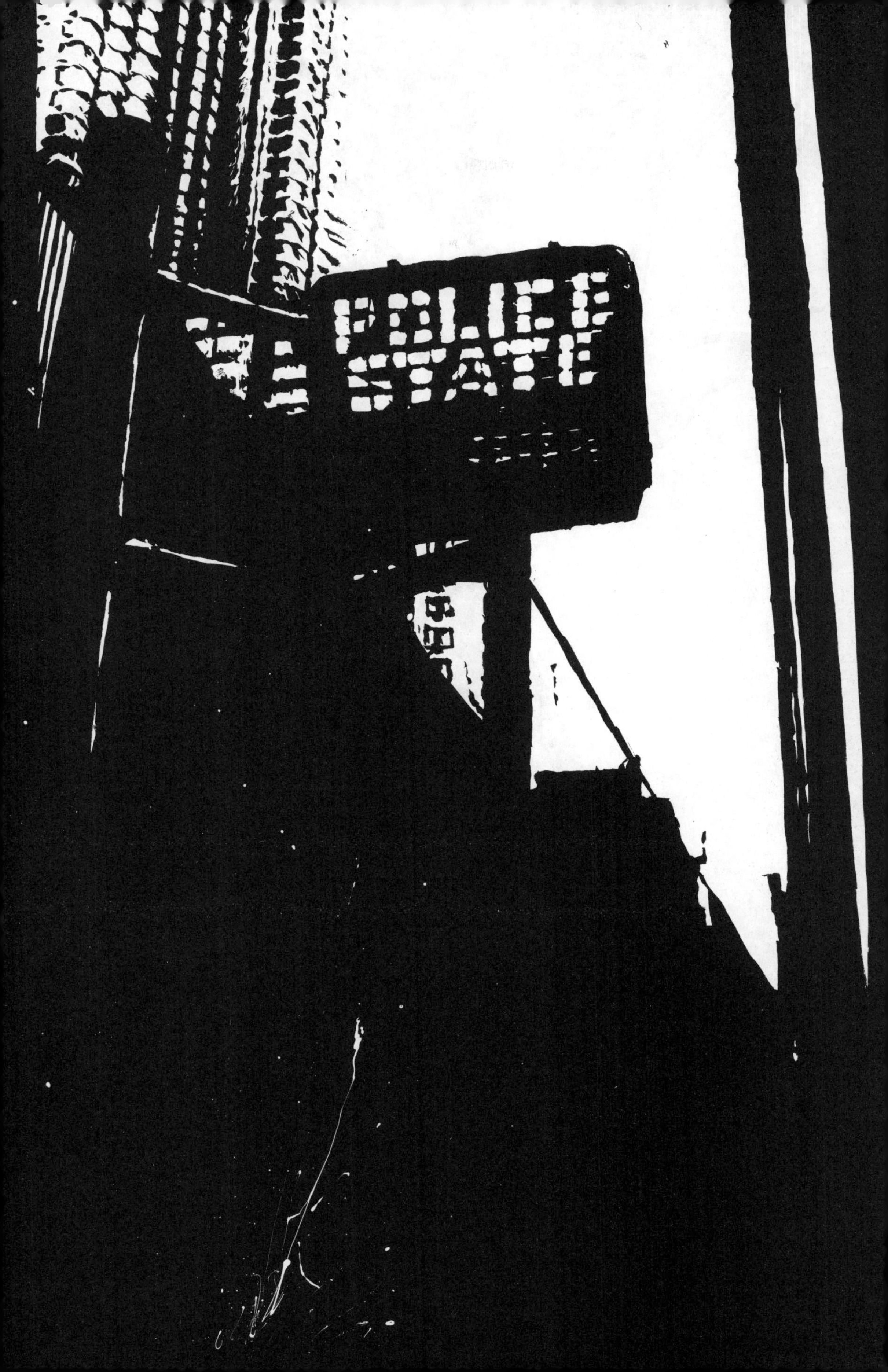
POLICE
STATE

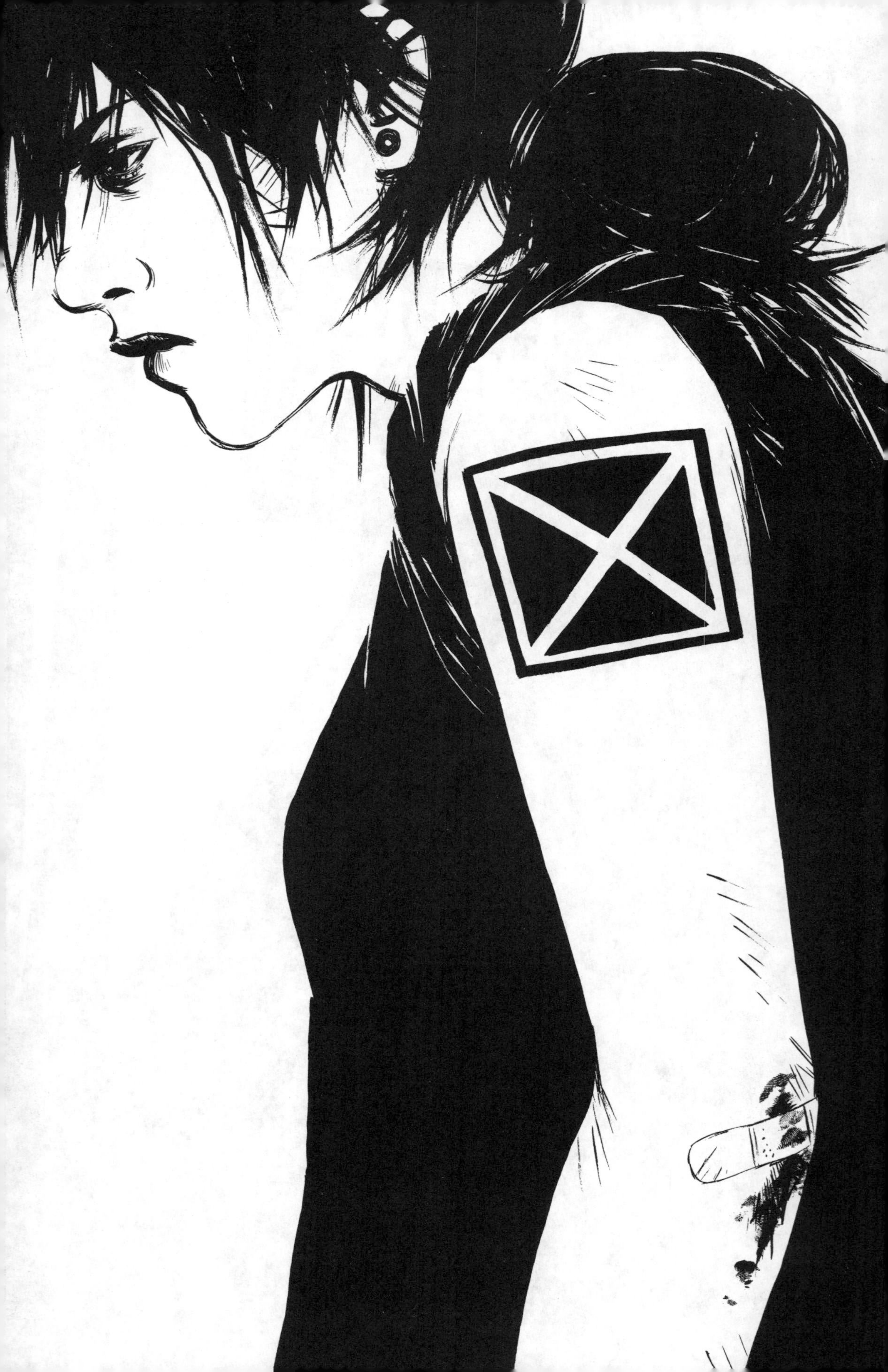

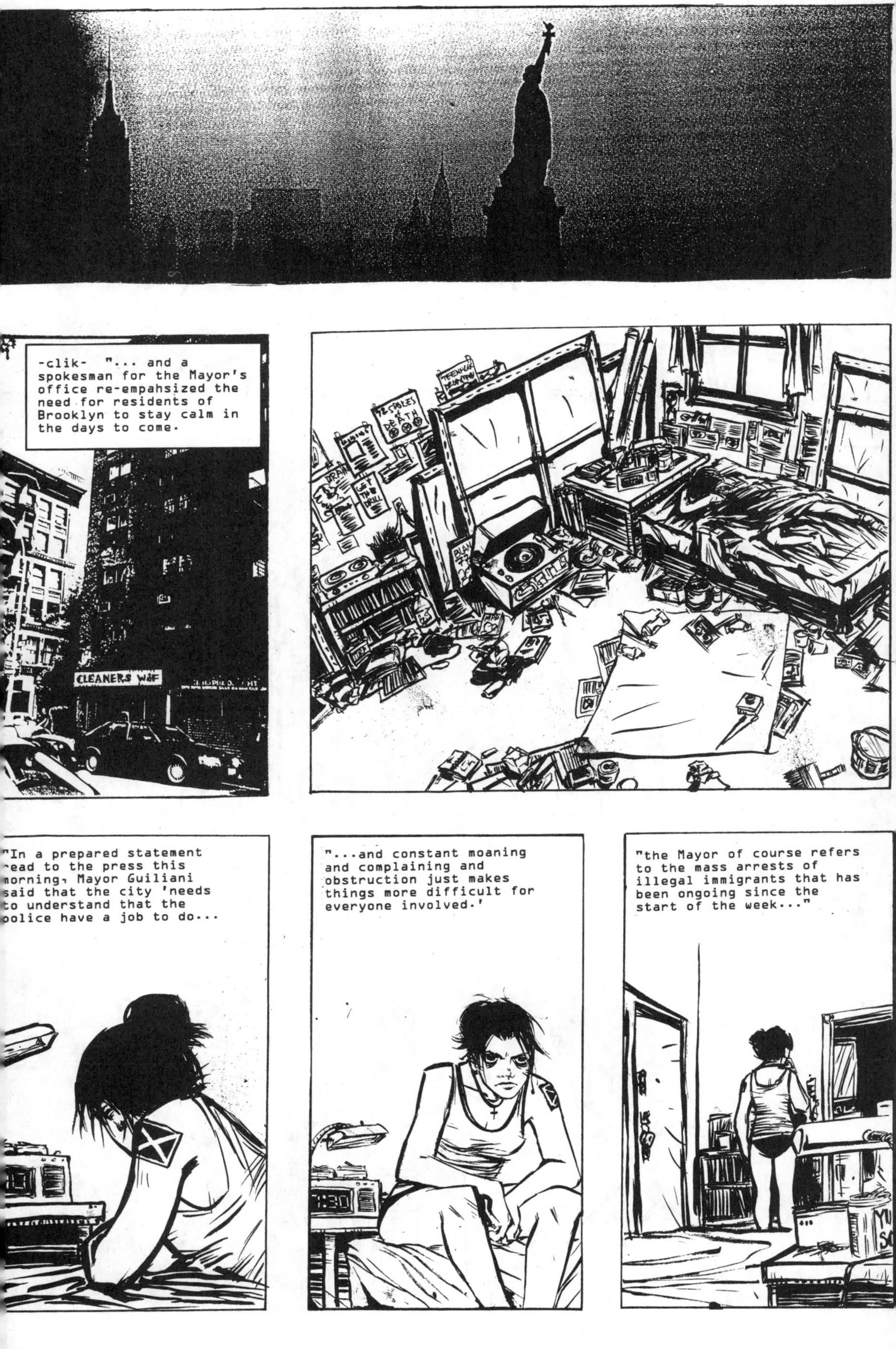
-clik- "... and a spokesman for the Mayor's office re-empahsized the need for residents of Brooklyn to stay calm in the days to come.
CLEANERS W&F
72 SPOKES of DEATH
GET THE DRILL
"In a prepared statement ead to the press this orning, Mayor Guiliani said that the city 'needs to understand that the olice have a job to do...
"...and constant moaning and complaining and obstruction just makes things more difficult for everyone involved.'
"the Mayor of course refers to the mass arrests of illegal immigrants that has been ongoing since the start of the week..."

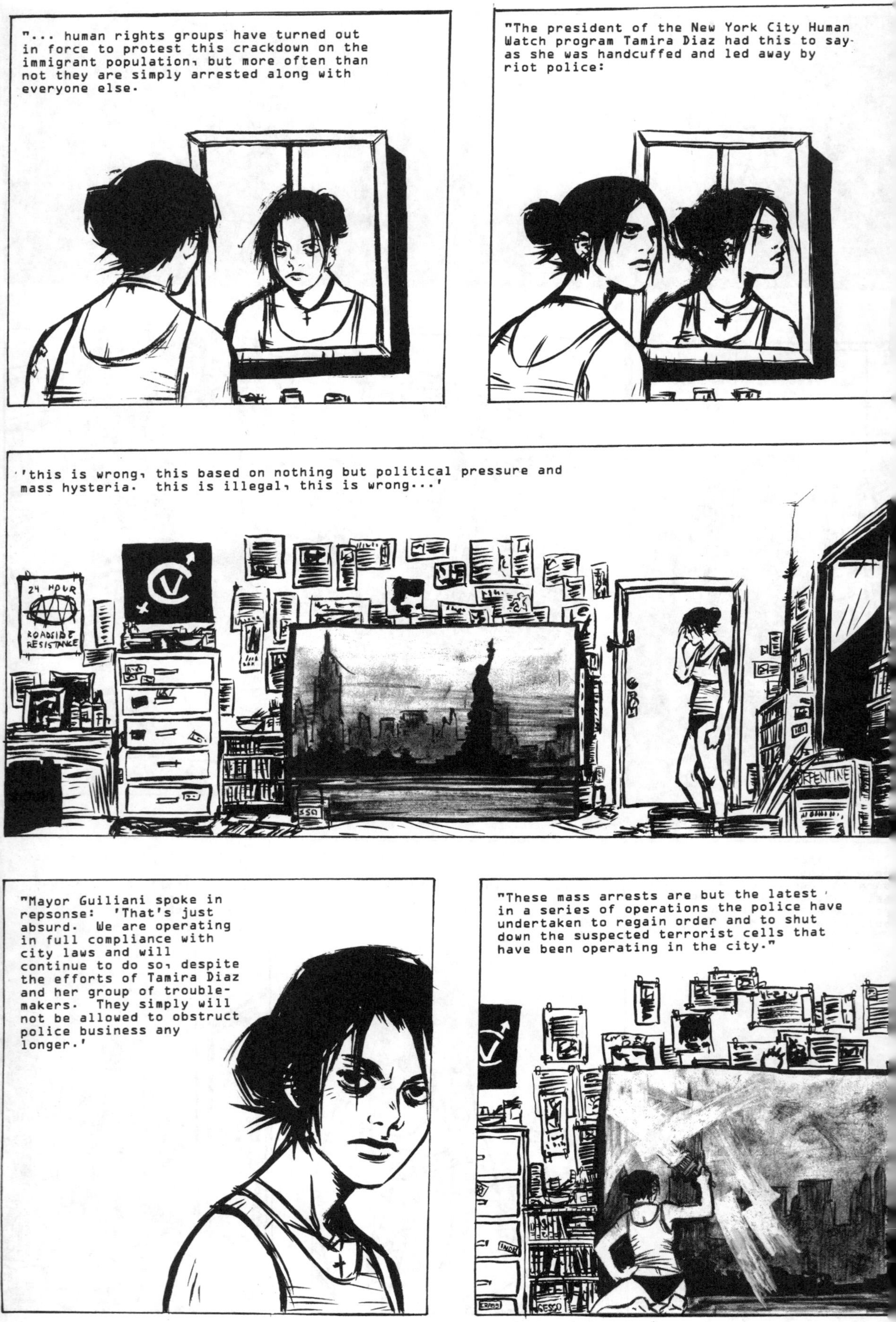
"... human rights groups have turned out in force to protest this crackdown on the immigrant population, but more often than not they are simply arrested along with everyone else.
"The president of the New York City Human Watch program Tamira Diaz had this to say as she was handcuffed and led away by riot police:
'this is wrong, this based on nothing but political pressure and mass hysteria. this is illegal, this is wrong...'
24 HOUR
ROADSIDE RESISTANCE
"Mayor Guiliani spoke in repsonse: 'That's just absurd. We are operating in full compliance with city laws and will continue to do so, despite the efforts of Tamira Diaz and her group of trouble-makers. They simply will not be allowed to obstruct police business any longer.'
"These mass arrests are but the latest in a series of operations the police have undertaken to regain order and to shut down the suspected terrorist cells that have been operating in the city."

"... the mayor went on to add: 'This city has a long history of dissent and cultural tolerance, and that history has led us to the point we're at now. Look outside your windows. Is this the environment you want to live in? To raise your children in? Are you proud of this city of ours?

"'I for one am not. And I won't allow this city I love to sink lower and lower each day. I will restore it to its former beauty and glory, and make a New York City a place we can all be proud of again.'

"The Mayor refused to elaborate on his use of the term 'cultural tolerance', adding, and i quote: 'You all know what it means.'"

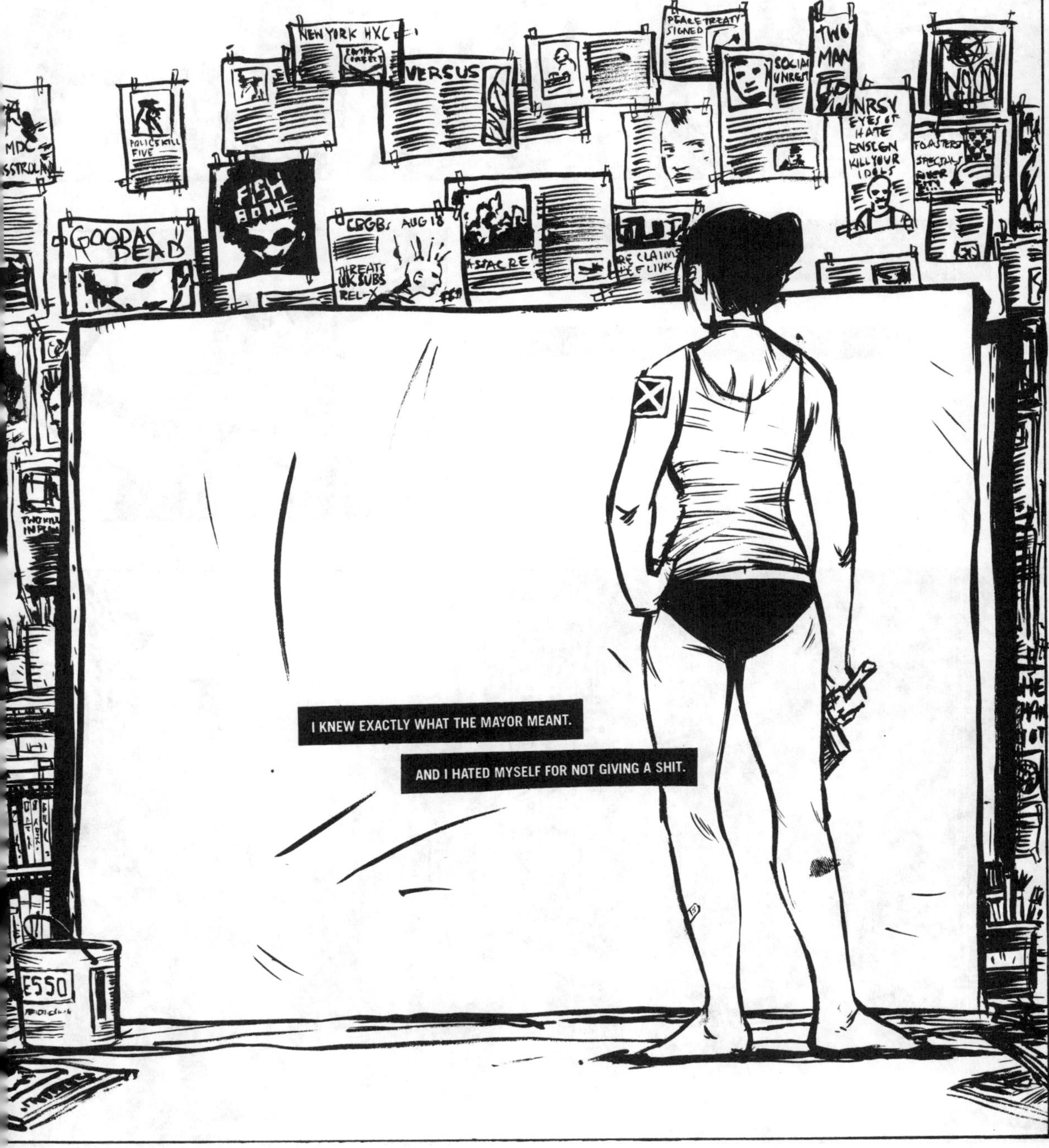
NEW YORK HXC
VERSUS
PEACE TREATY SIGNED
TWO MAN
SOCIAL UNREST
EYES OF HATE
ENSIGN
KILL YOUR IDOLS
POLICE KILL FIVE
FISH BONE
GOOD AS DEAD
CBGB AUG 18
UK SUBS
REL-X
ESSO
I KNEW EXACTLY WHAT THE MAYOR MEANT.
AND I HATED MYSELF FOR NOT GIVING A SHIT.

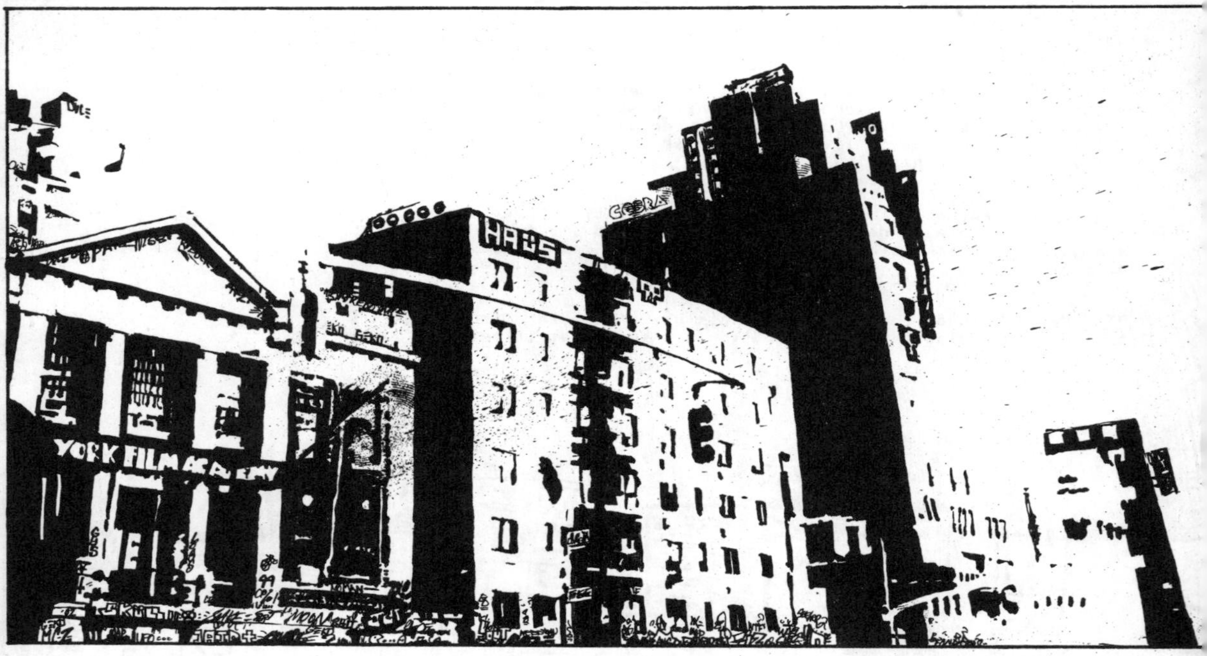
YORK FILM ACADEMY
HAUS
COBRA

THOSE EARLY CLASSES WERE HORRIBLE. THE FREAKS AND PERVERTS AND ACTIVISTS AND COPS WERE ALWAYS OUT IN FORCE IN THE MORNINGS, BEFORE IT GOT TOO HOT.

LOOKING BACK, IT'S A WONDER I DIDN'T FREAK OUT MYSELF.

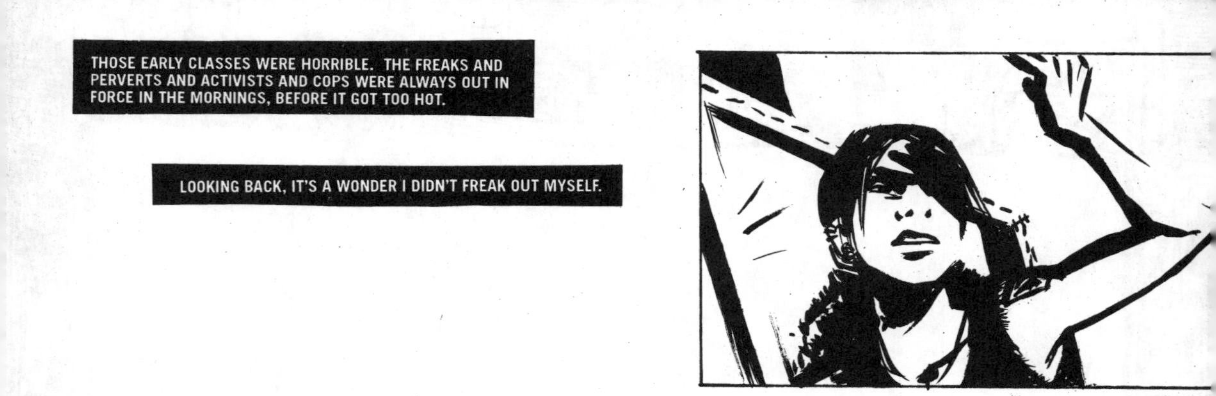

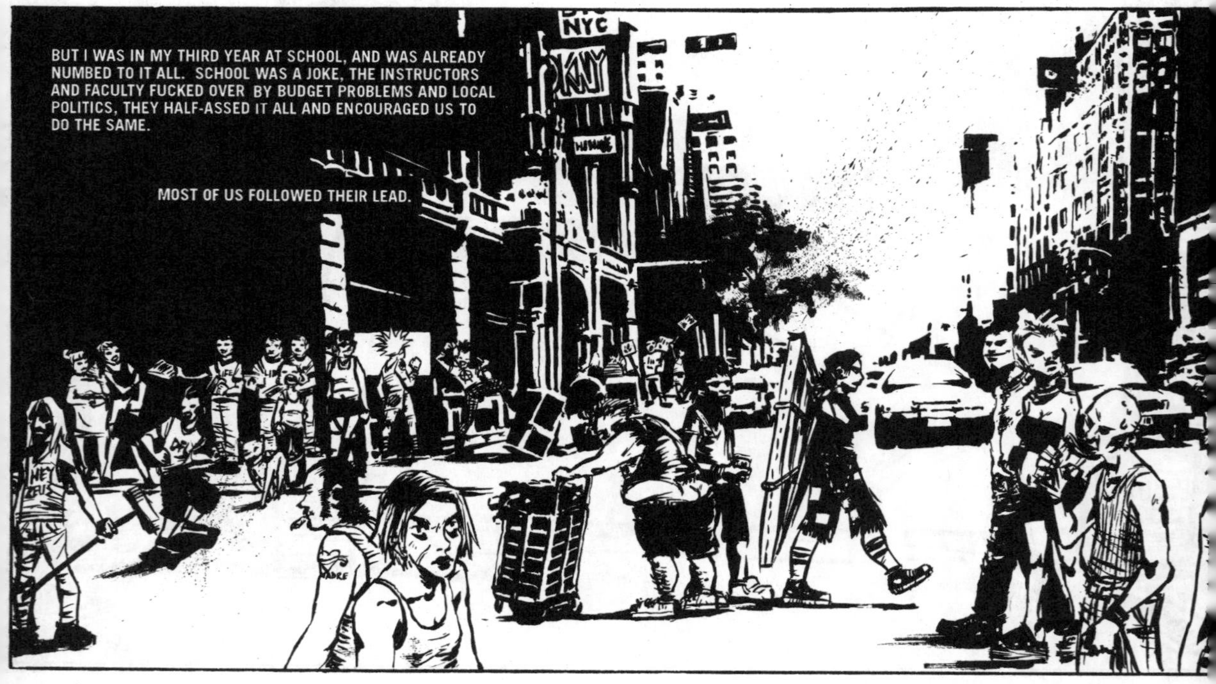
BUT I WAS IN MY THIRD YEAR AT SCHOOL, AND WAS ALREADY NUMBED TO IT ALL. SCHOOL WAS A JOKE, THE INSTRUCTORS AND FACULTY FUCKED OVER BY BUDGET PROBLEMS AND LOCAL POLITICS, THEY HALF-ASSED IT ALL AND ENCOURAGED US TO DO THE SAME.
MOST OF US FOLLOWED THEIR LEAD.
NYC
DKNY

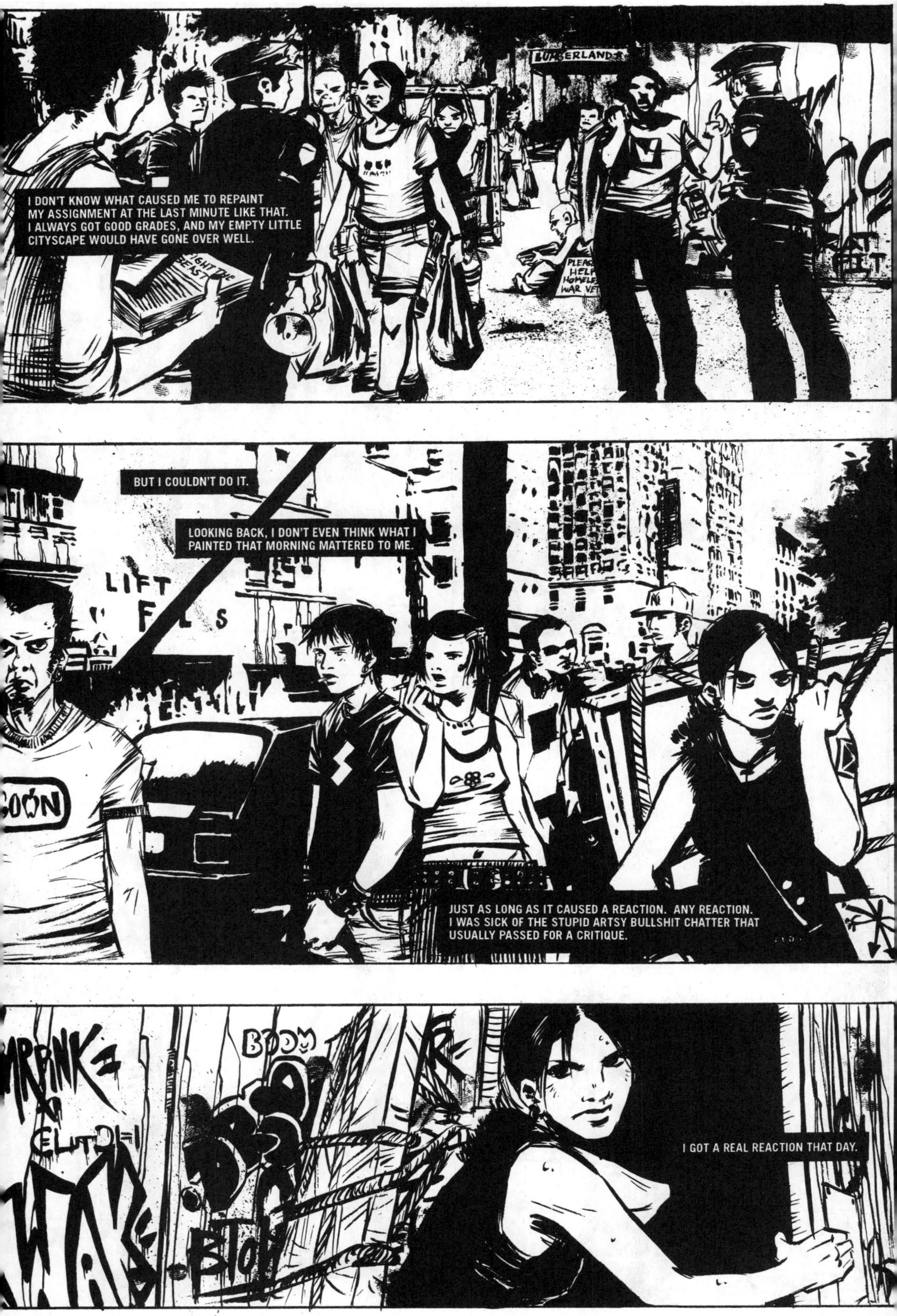
BUMBERLAND
I DON'T KNOW WHAT CAUSED ME TO REPAINT MY ASSIGNMENT AT THE LAST MINUTE LIKE THAT. I ALWAYS GOT GOOD GRADES, AND MY EMPTY LITTLE CITYSCAPE WOULD HAVE GONE OVER WELL.
BUT I COULDN'T DO IT.
LOOKING BACK, I DON'T EVEN THINK WHAT I PAINTED THAT MORNING MATTERED TO ME.
LIFT
GOON
JUST AS LONG AS IT CAUSED A REACTION. ANY REACTION. I WAS SICK OF THE STUPID ARTSY BULLSHIT CHATTER THAT USUALLY PASSED FOR A CRITIQUE.
BOOM
I GOT A REAL REACTION THAT DAY.

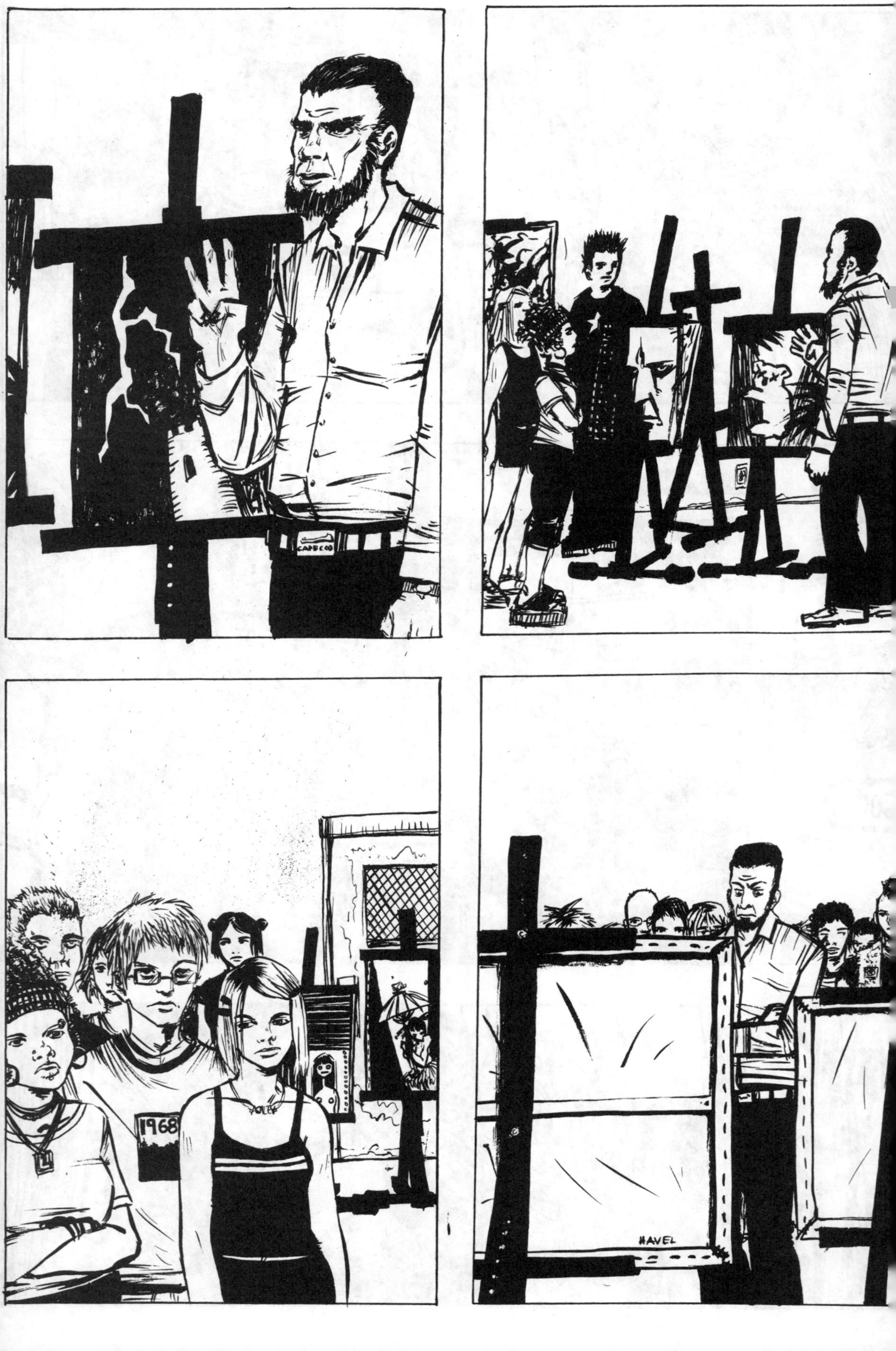
1968
HAVEL

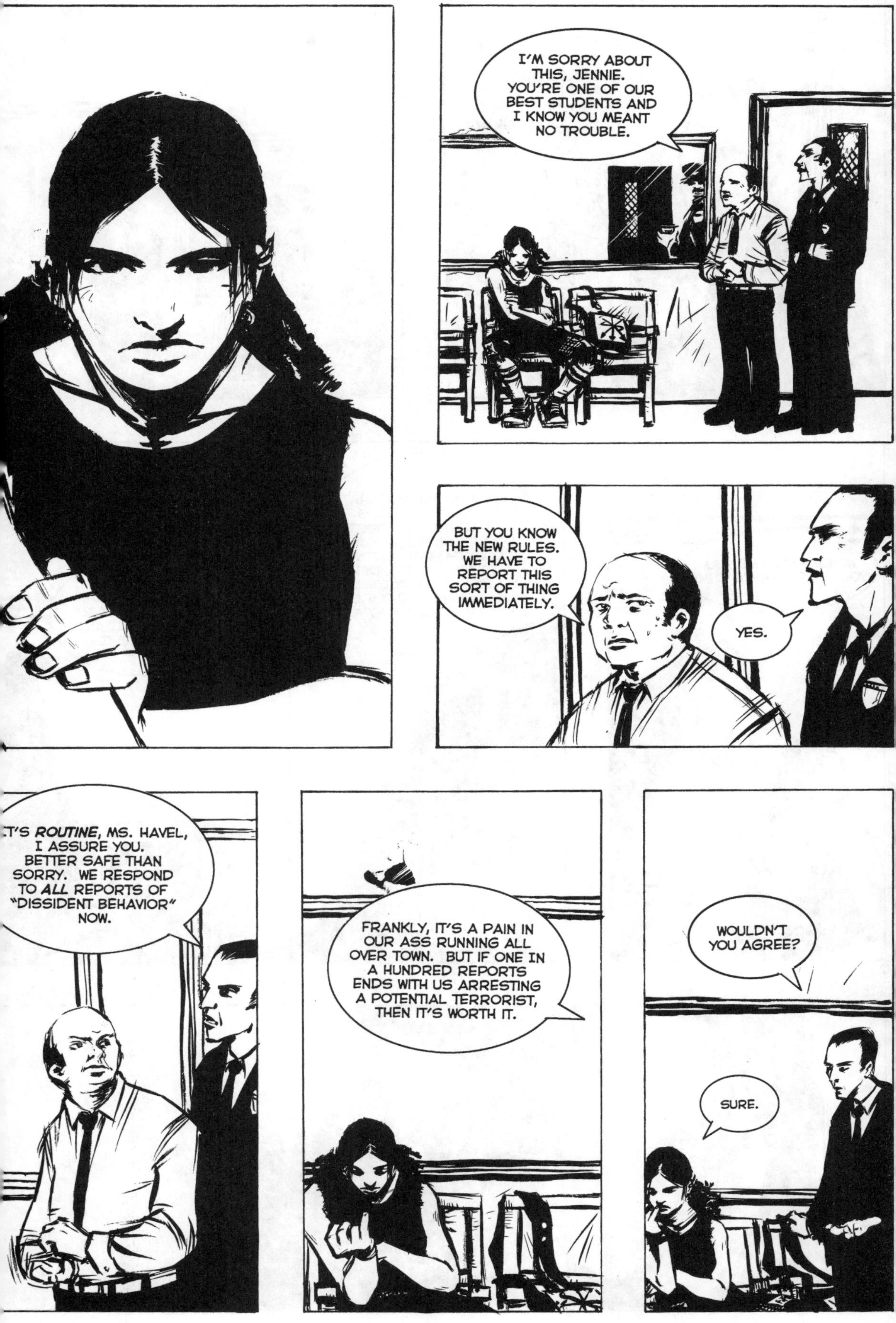
I'M SORRY ABOUT THIS, JENNIE. YOU'RE ONE OF OUR BEST STUDENTS AND I KNOW YOU MEANT NO TROUBLE.
BUT YOU KNOW THE NEW RULES. WE HAVE TO REPORT THIS SORT OF THING IMMEDIATELY.
YES.
IT'S *ROUTINE*, MS. HAVEL, I ASSURE YOU. BETTER SAFE THAN SORRY. WE RESPOND TO *ALL* REPORTS OF "DISSIDENT BEHAVIOR" NOW.
FRANKLY, IT'S A PAIN IN OUR ASS RUNNING ALL OVER TOWN. BUT IF ONE IN A HUNDRED REPORTS ENDS WITH US ARRESTING A POTENTIAL TERRORIST, THEN IT'S WORTH IT.
WOULDN'T YOU AGREE?
SURE.

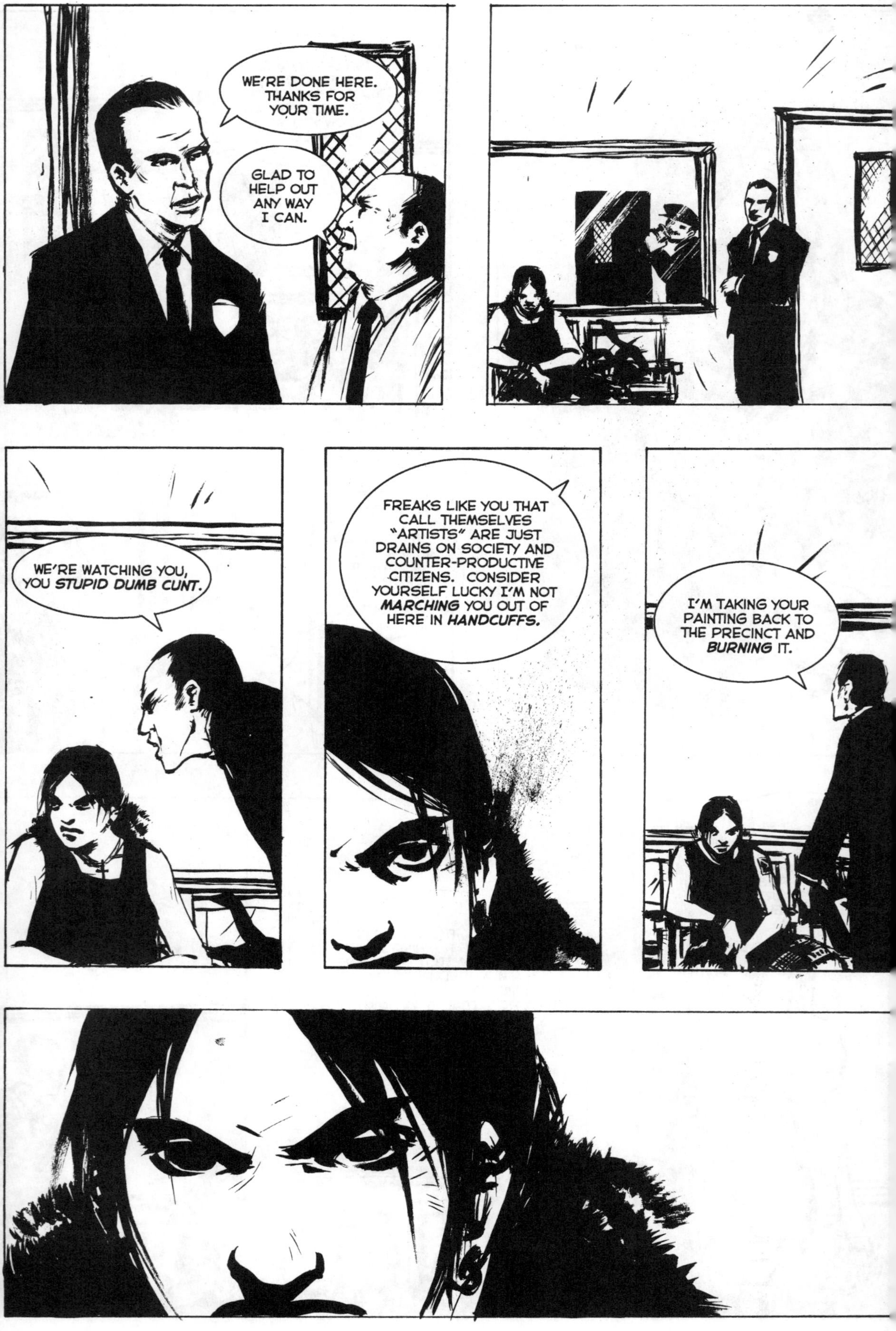
WE'RE DONE HERE. THANKS FOR YOUR TIME.
GLAD TO HELP OUT ANY WAY I CAN.
WE'RE WATCHING YOU, YOU STUPID DUMB CUNT.
FREAKS LIKE YOU THAT CALL THEMSELVES "ARTISTS" ARE JUST DRAINS ON SOCIETY AND COUNTER-PRODUCTIVE CITIZENS. CONSIDER YOURSELF LUCKY I'M NOT MARCHING YOU OUT OF HERE IN HANDCUFFS.
I'M TAKING YOUR PAINTING BACK TO THE PRECINCT AND BURNING IT.

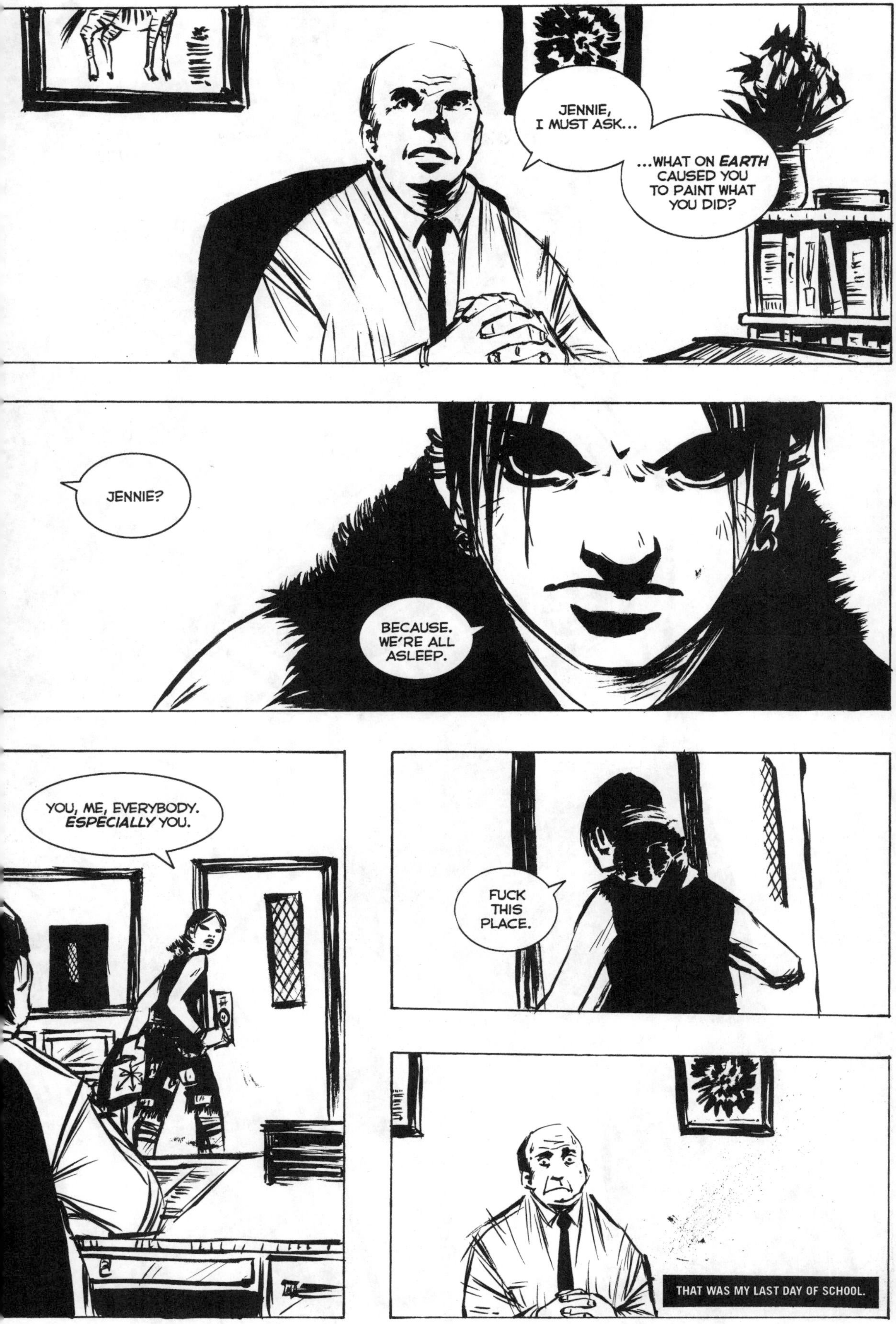
JENNIE, I MUST ASK...
...WHAT ON *EARTH* CAUSED YOU TO PAINT WHAT YOU DID?
JENNIE?
BECAUSE. WE'RE ALL ASLEEP.
YOU, ME, EVERYBODY. *ESPECIALLY* YOU.
FUCK THIS PLACE.
THAT WAS MY LAST DAY OF SCHOOL.

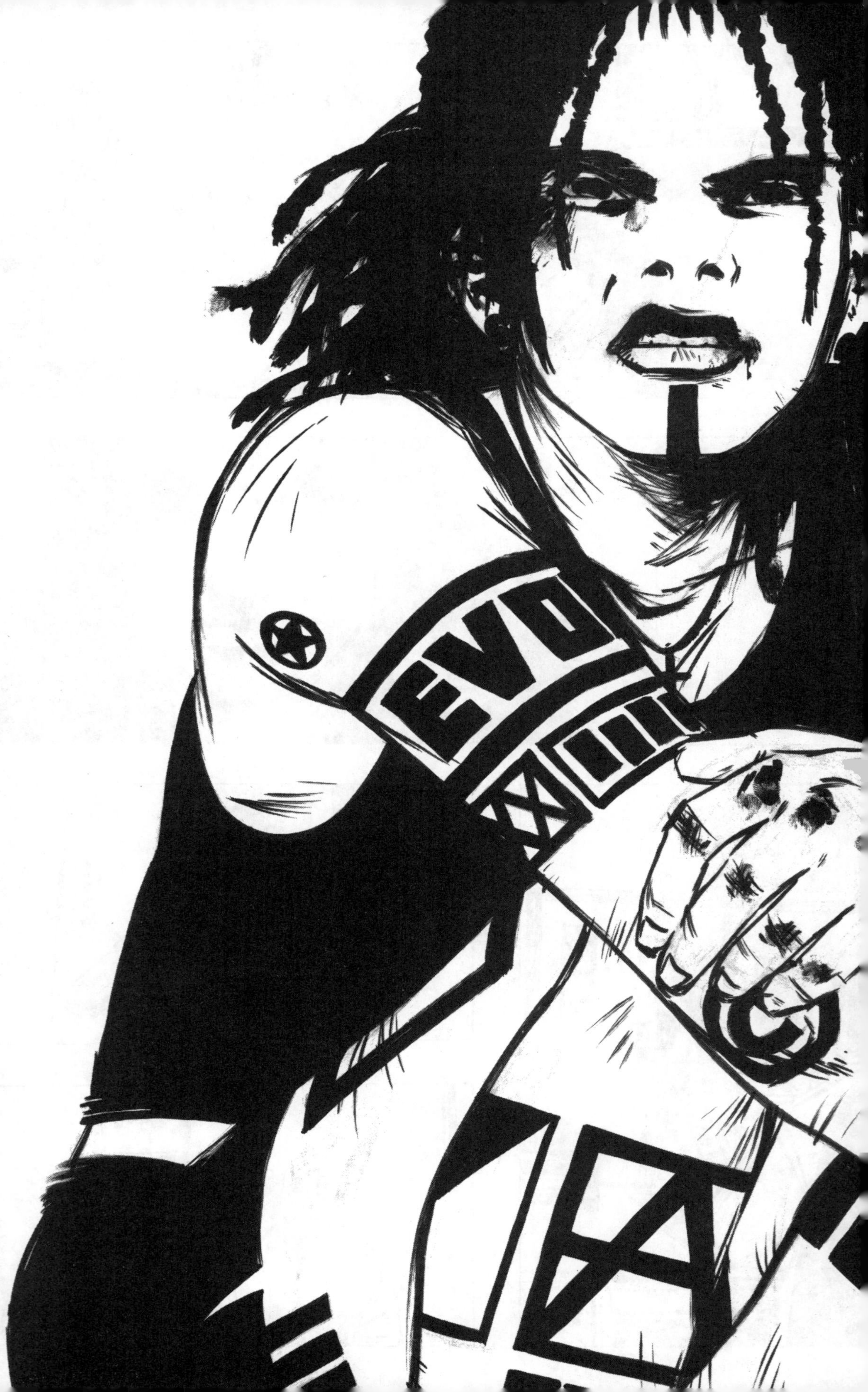
EVO

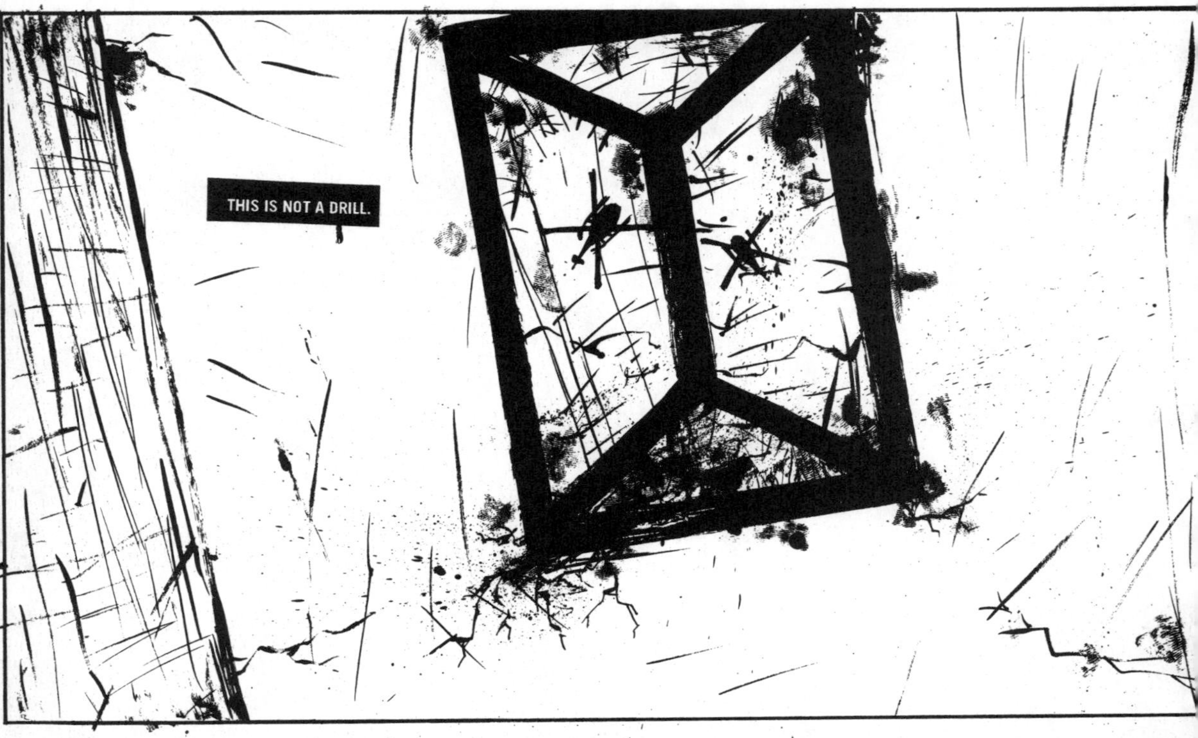
THIS IS NOT A DRILL.

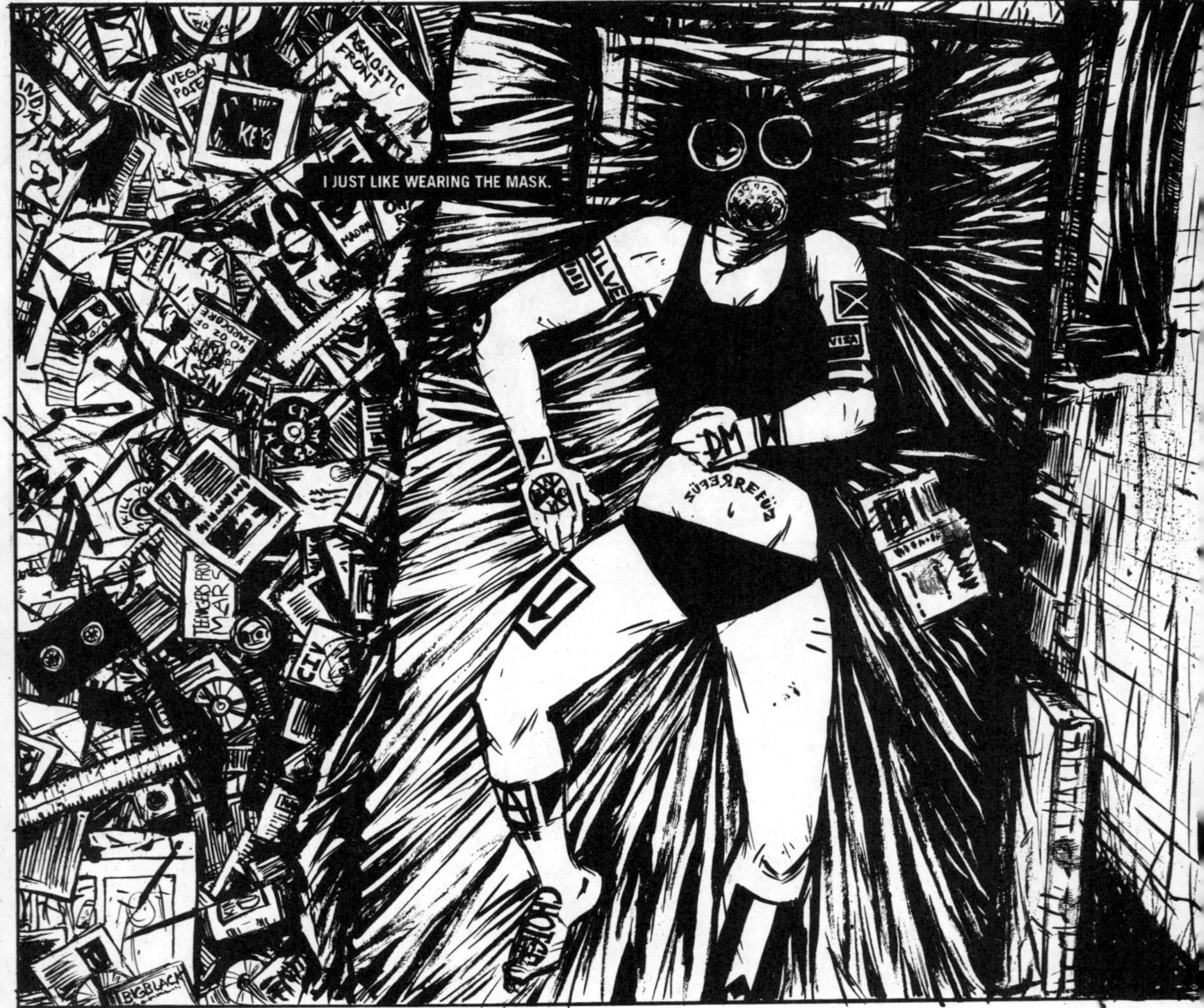
I JUST LIKE WEARING THE MASK.

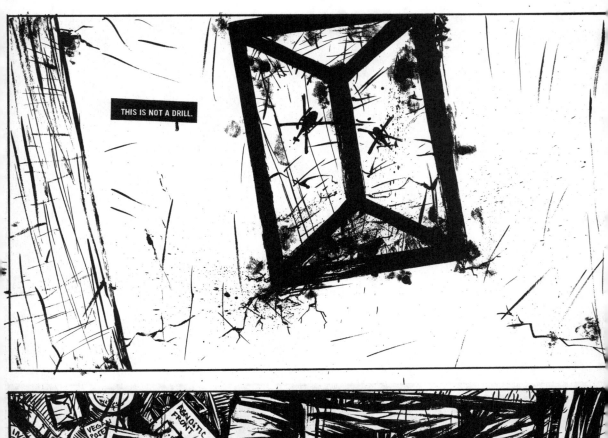

I BOUGHT IT WHEN I WAS TWELVE YEARS OLD FROM THE ARMY/NAVY, BECAUSE I THOUGHT IT LOOKED COOL AND PUNK ROCK AND NO ONE ELSE HAD ONE. IT COST ME FIFTEEN BUCKS.

NOW EVERYONE HAS ONE. THE PARANOID PEOPLE ANYWAY, AND THAT'S A LOT OF PEOPLE THESE DAYS. IF I TRIED TO GO BUY ONE RIGHT NOW, IF I WAS LUCKY TO FIND ONE, I BET IT WOULD COSTS HUNDREDS.

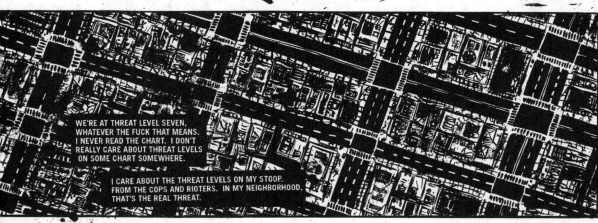

WE'RE AT THREAT LEVEL SEVEN, WHATEVER THE FUCK THAT MEANS. I NEVER READ THE CHART. I DON'T REALLY CARE ABOUT THREAT LEVELS ON SOME CHART SOMEWHERE.

I CARE ABOUT THE THREAT LEVELS ON MY STOOP. FROM THE COPS AND RIOTERS. IN MY NEIGHBORHOOD, THAT'S THE REAL THREAT.

WE'RE SUPPOSED TO BE "UNDER ATTACK" FROM THE "BAD GUYS". IMMIGRANTS, EXCHANGE STUDENTS, LEADERS OF FOREIGN COUNTRIES, THAT SORT OF THING.

OUR CITY, AND THE REST OF THE COUNTRY, IS SPENDING SO MUCH TIME AND MONEY PROTECTING US FROM THEM, THEY FORGET TO PROTECT US FROM EACH OTHER.

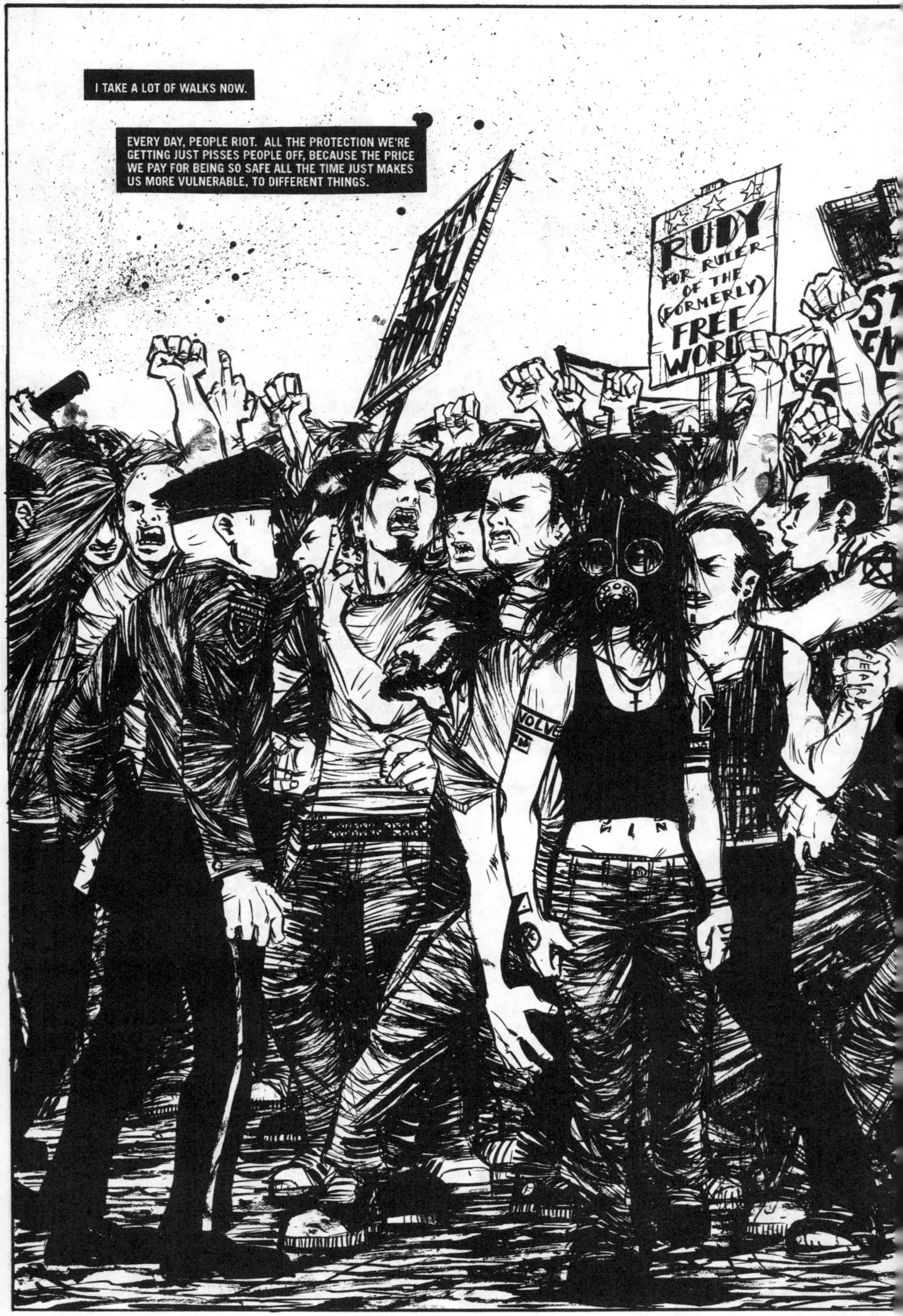
I TAKE A LOT OF WALKS NOW.
EVERY DAY, PEOPLE RIOT. ALL THE PROTECTION WE'RE GETTING JUST PISSES PEOPLE OFF, BECAUSE THE PRICE WE PAY FOR BEING SO SAFE ALL THE TIME JUST MAKES US MORE VULNERABLE, TO DIFFERENT THINGS.
RUDY
FOR RULER
OF THE
(FORMERLY)
FREE

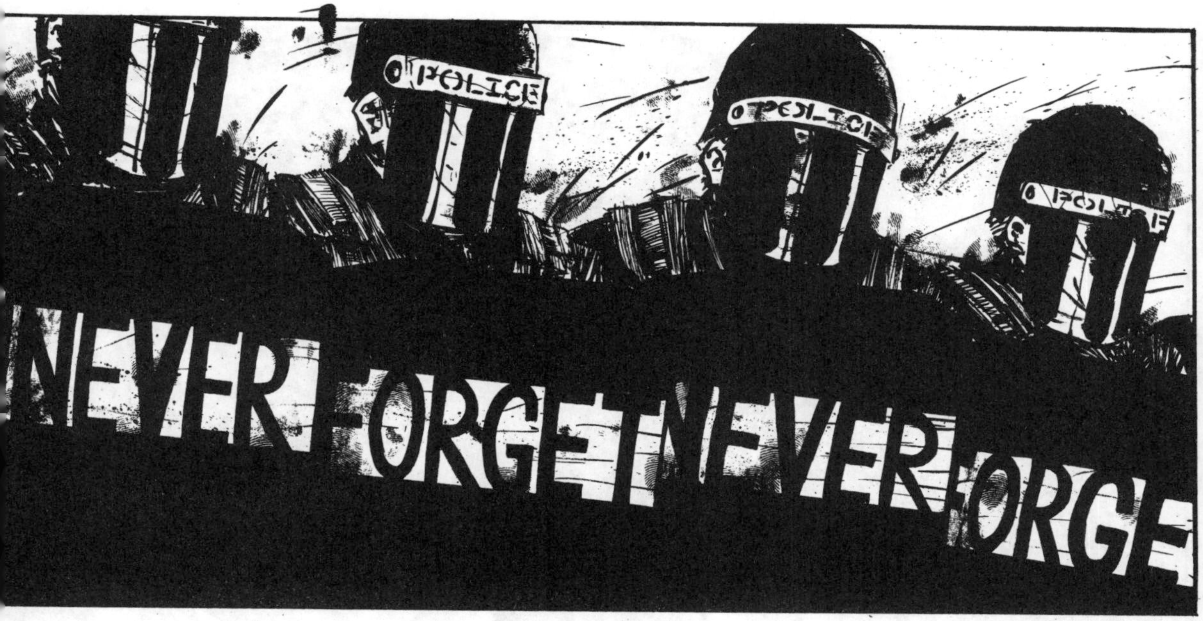
POLICE
NEVER FORGET NEVER FORGE

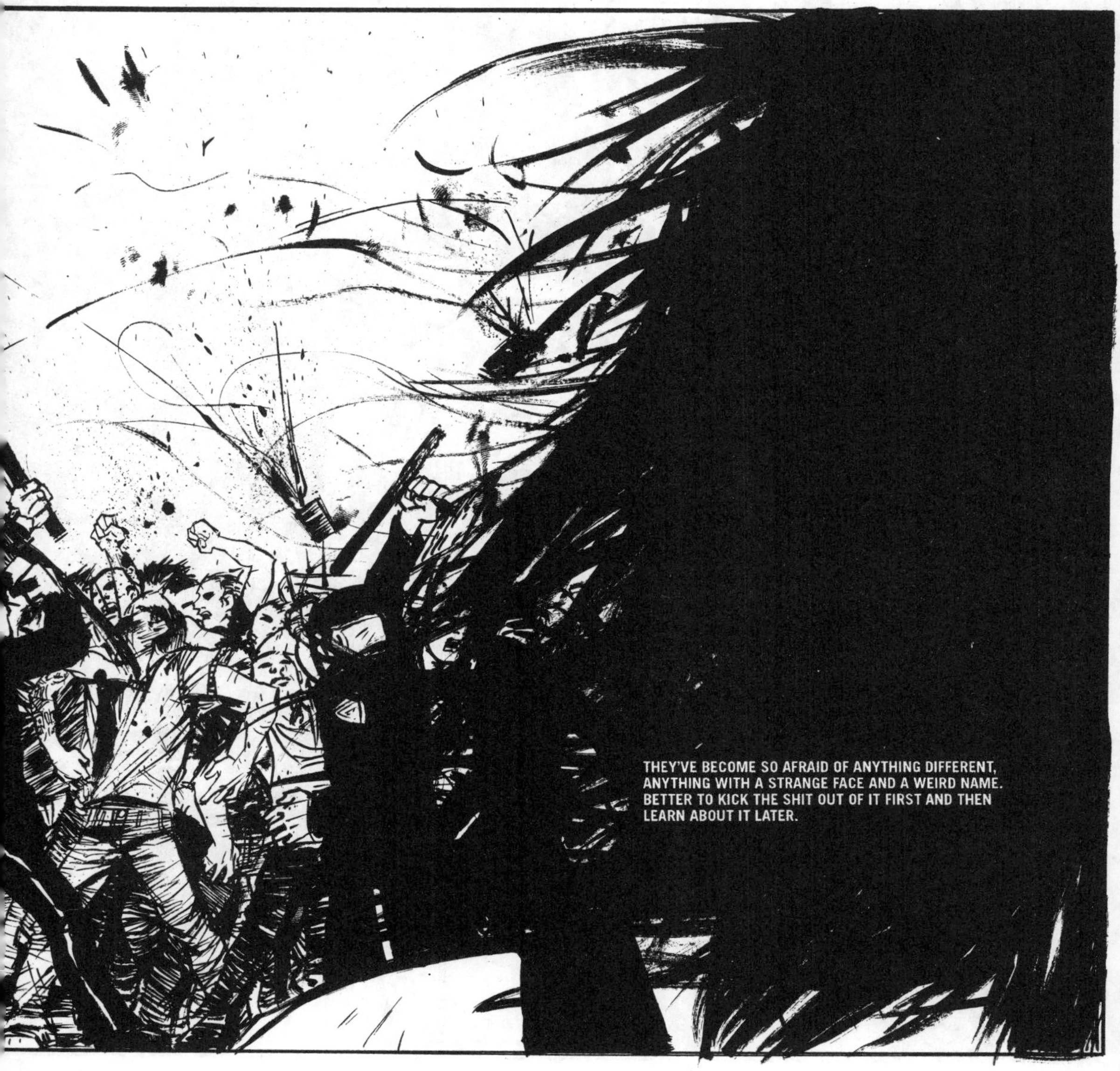
THEY'VE BECOME SO AFRAID OF ANYTHING DIFFERENT, ANYTHING WITH A STRANGE FACE AND A WEIRD NAME. BETTER TO KICK THE SHIT OUT OF IT FIRST AND THEN LEARN ABOUT IT LATER.

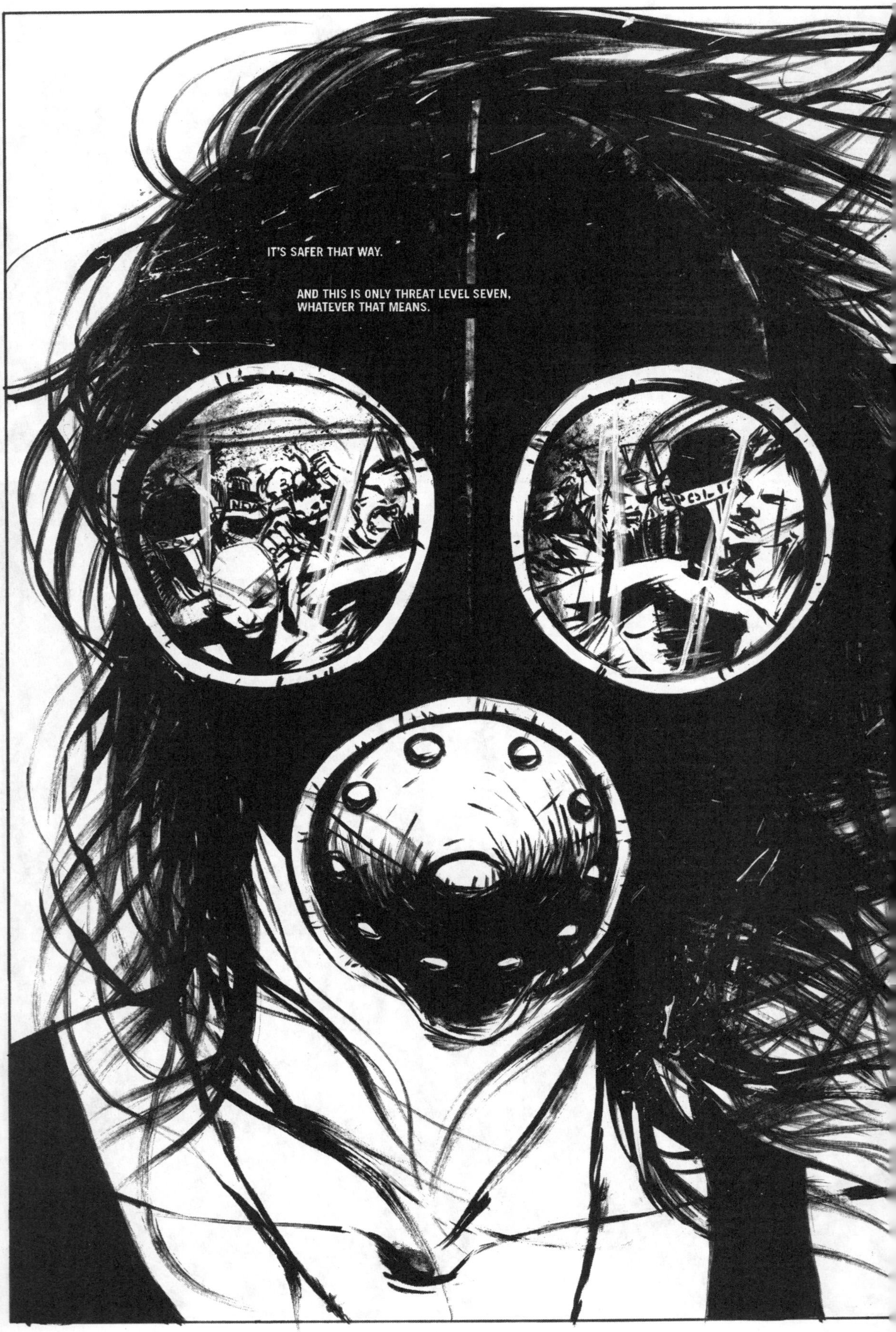
IT'S SAFER THAT WAY.
AND THIS IS ONLY THREAT LEVEL SEVEN, WHATEVER THAT MEANS.

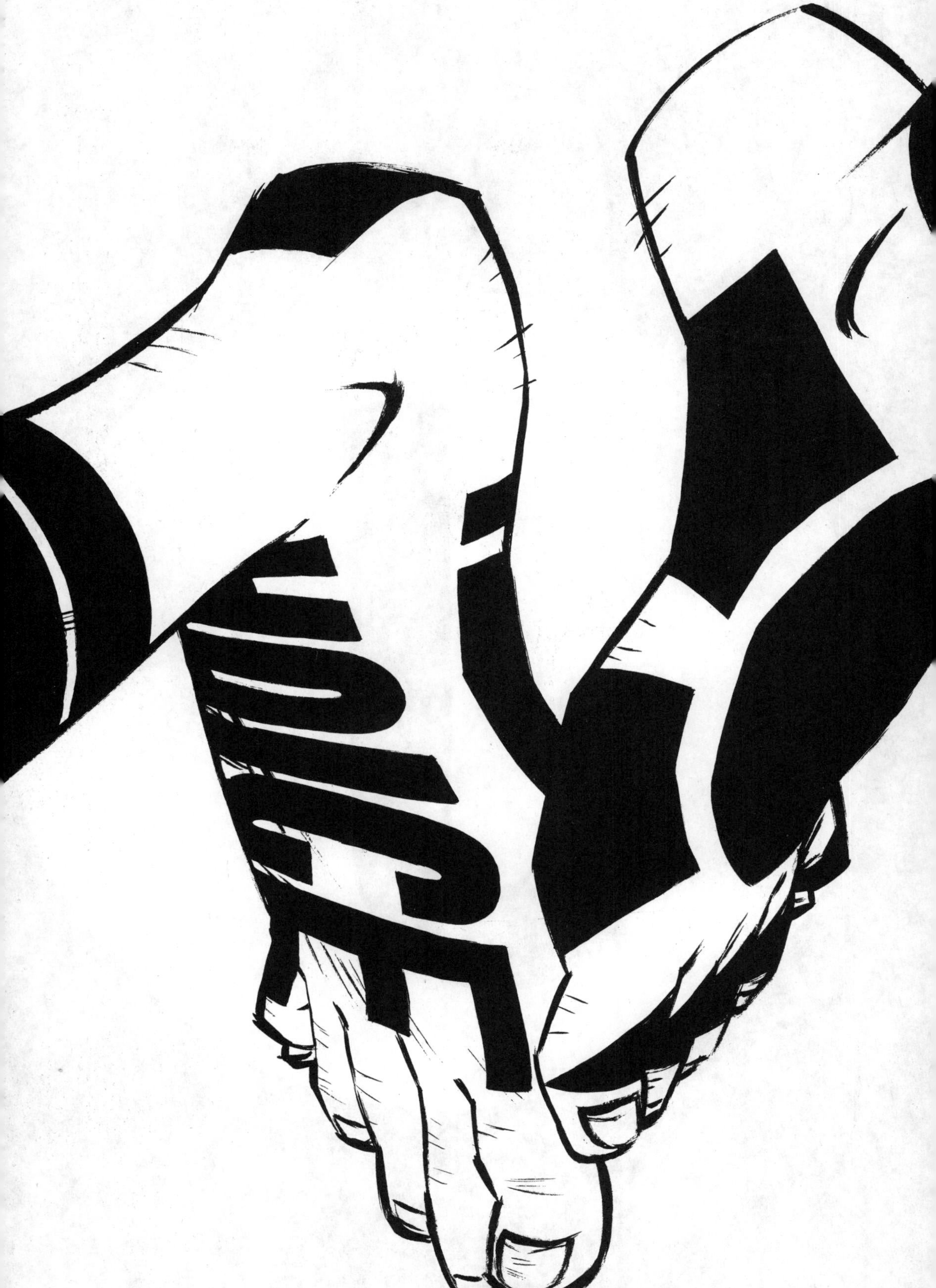

J

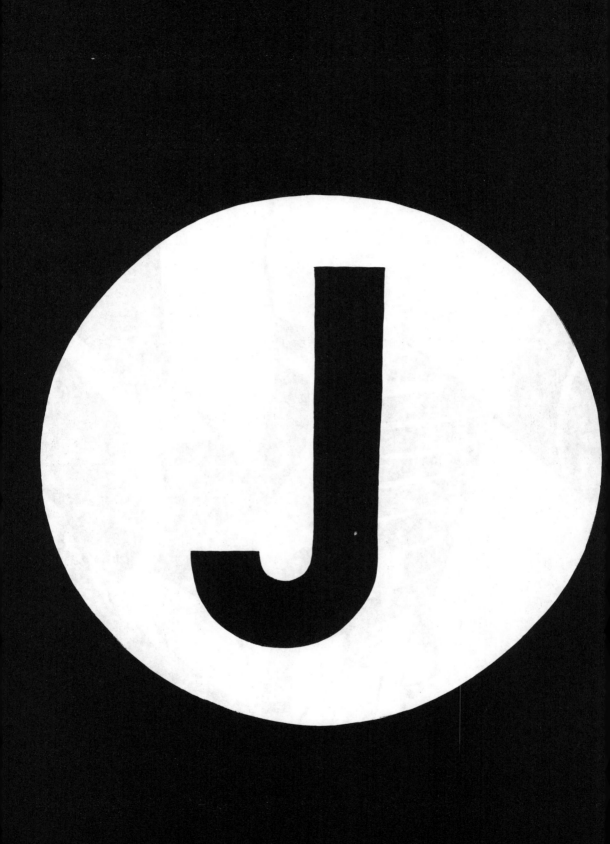

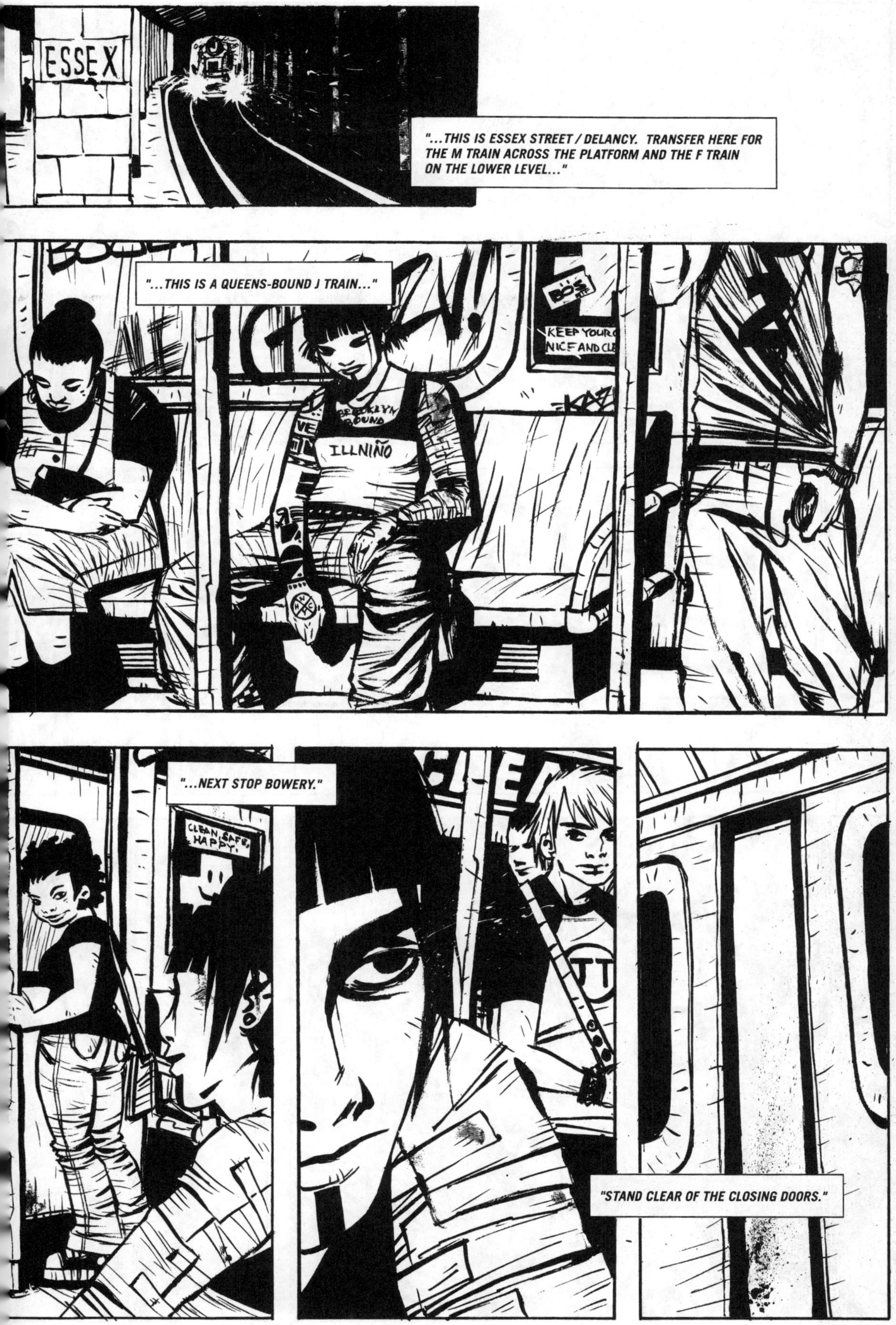
ESSEX
"...THIS IS ESSEX STREET / DELANCY. TRANSFER HERE FOR THE M TRAIN ACROSS THE PLATFORM AND THE F TRAIN ON THE LOWER LEVEL..."
"...THIS IS A QUEENS-BOUND J TRAIN..."
BROOKLYN BOUND
ILLNIÑO
"...NEXT STOP BOWERY."
CLEAN, SAFE, HAPPY.
"STAND CLEAR OF THE CLOSING DOORS."

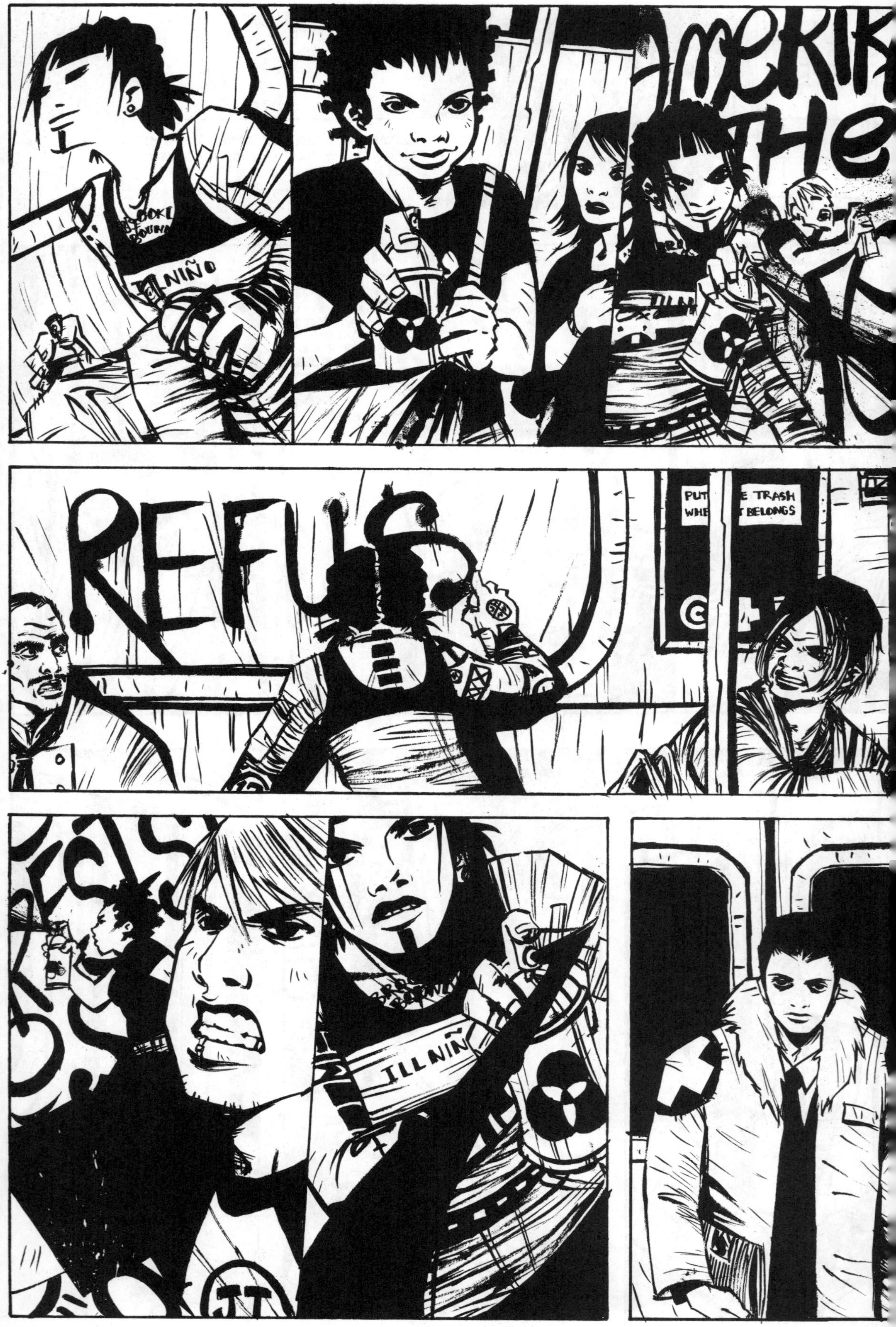

ILL NIÑO
AMERIK
THE
REFUS
PUT E TRASH
WHE T BELONGS
ILL NIÑ

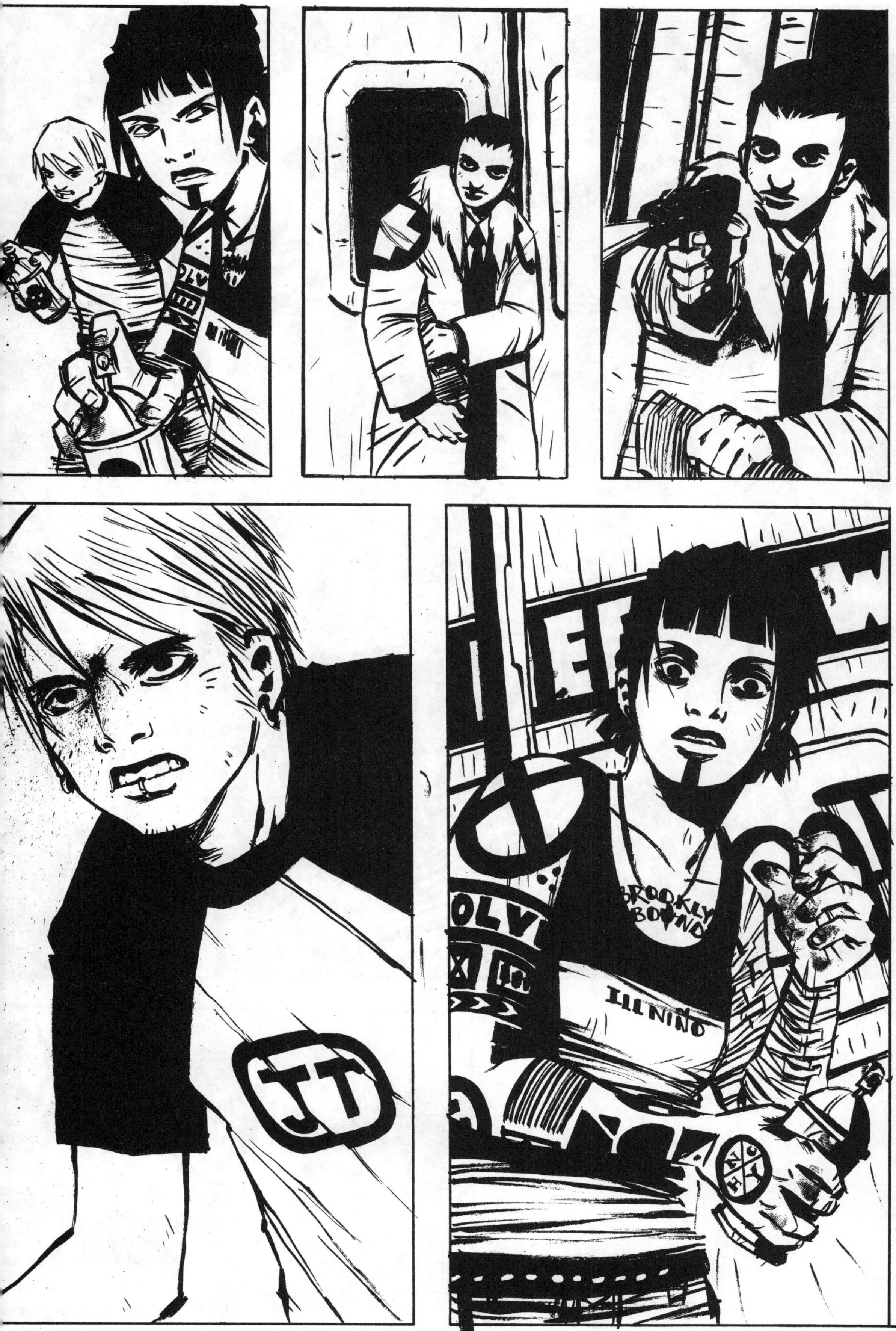
JT
ILL NIÑO

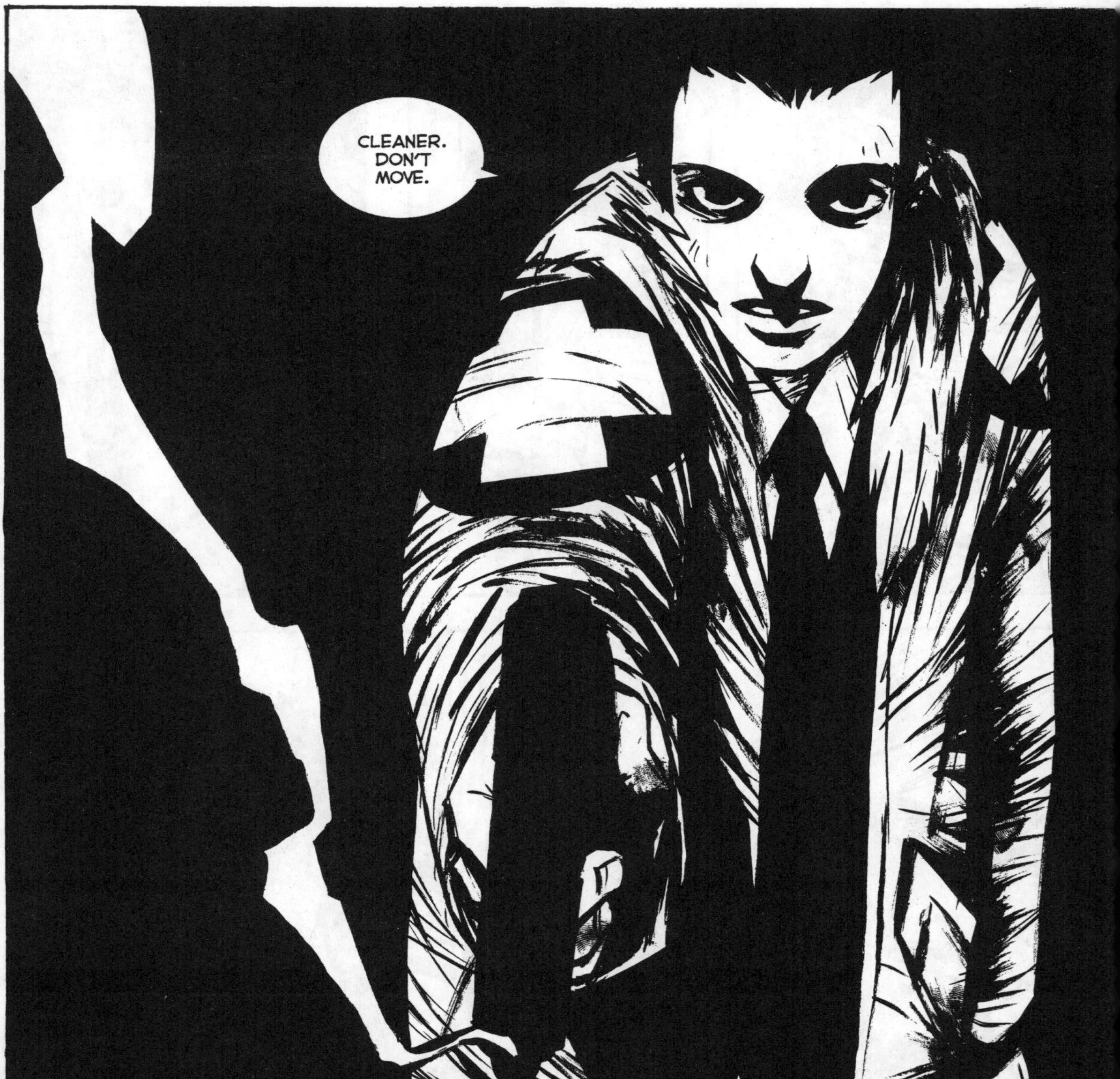
CLEANER.
DON'T
MOVE.

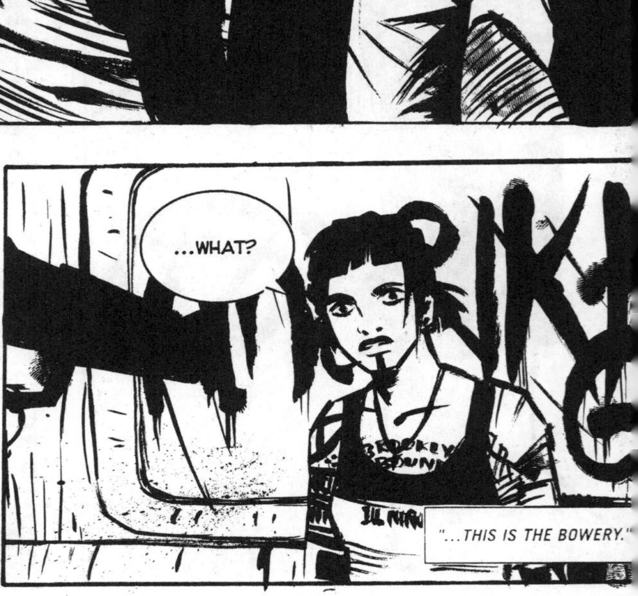
...WHAT?
"...THIS IS THE BOWERY."

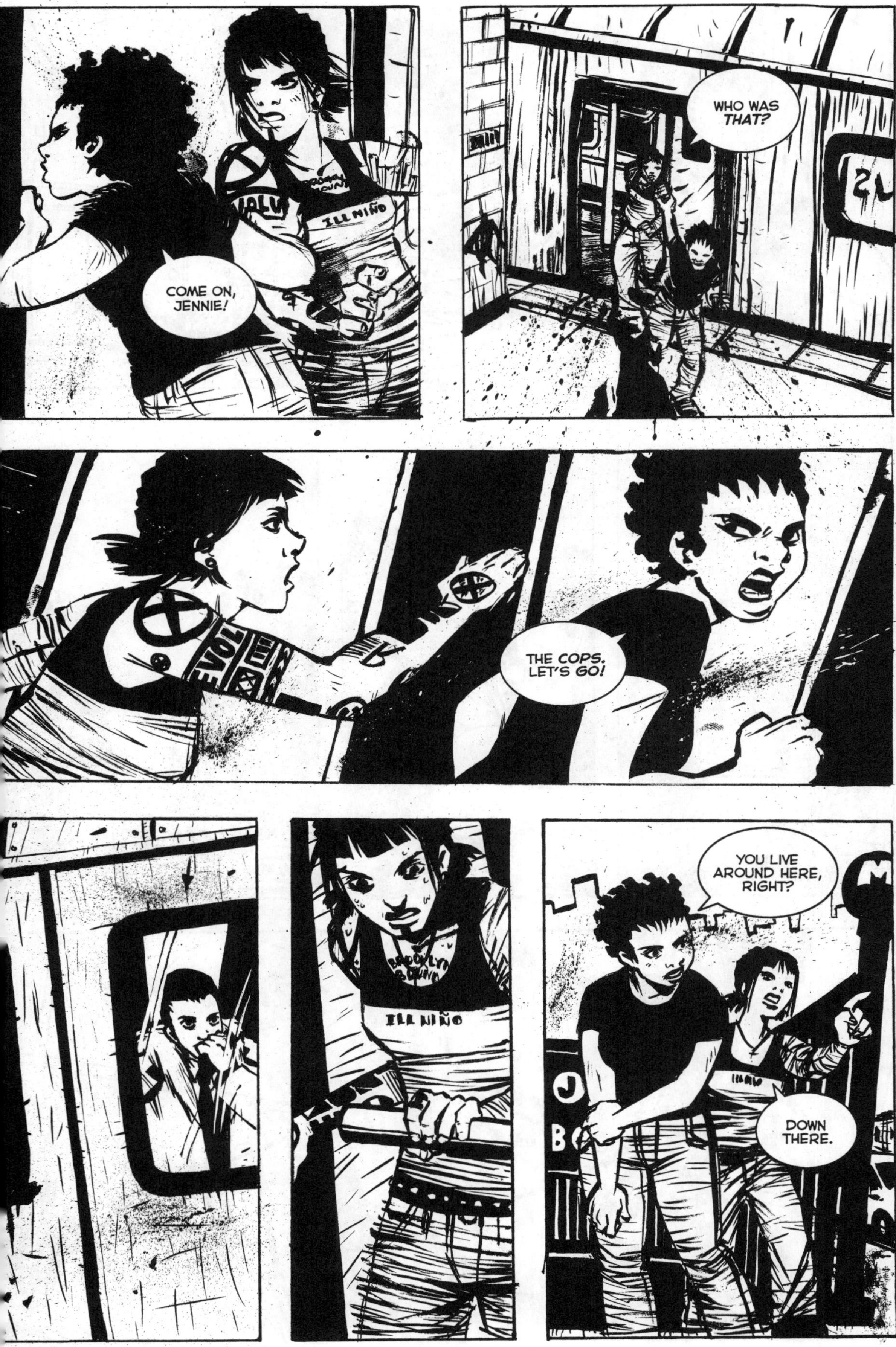
COME ON, JENNIE!
WHO WAS THAT?
THE COPS. LET'S GO!
YOU LIVE AROUND HERE, RIGHT?
DOWN THERE.

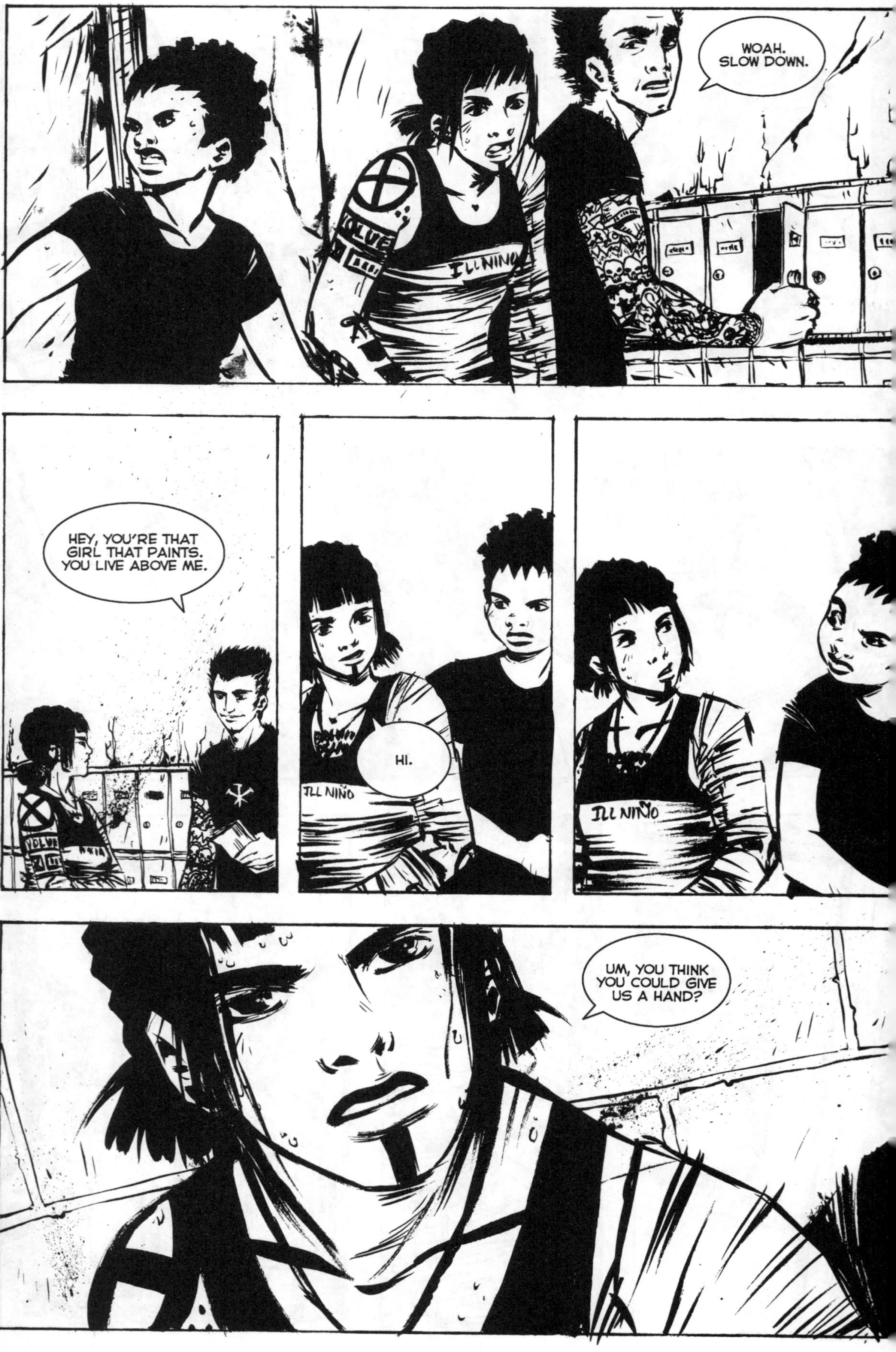
WOAH. SLOW DOWN.
ILL NIÑO
HEY, YOU'RE THAT GIRL THAT PAINTS. YOU LIVE ABOVE ME.
HI.
ILL NIÑO
ILL NIÑO
UM, YOU THINK YOU COULD GIVE US A HAND?

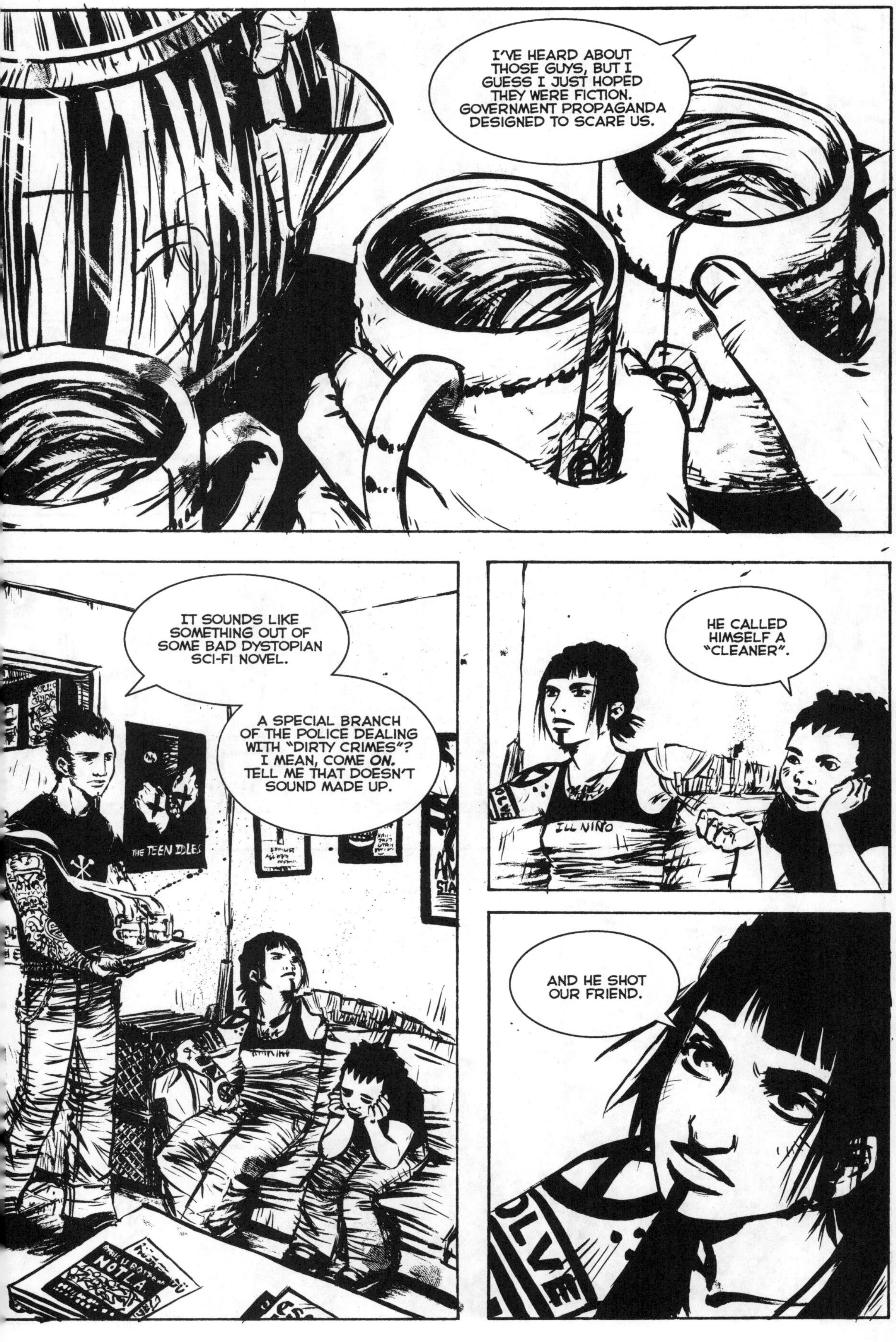
I'VE HEARD ABOUT THOSE GUYS, BUT I GUESS I JUST HOPED THEY WERE FICTION. GOVERNMENT PROPAGANDA DESIGNED TO SCARE US.
IT SOUNDS LIKE SOMETHING OUT OF SOME BAD DYSTOPIAN SCI-FI NOVEL.
A SPECIAL BRANCH OF THE POLICE DEALING WITH "DIRTY CRIMES"? I MEAN, COME *ON*. TELL ME THAT DOESN'T SOUND MADE UP.
THE TEEN IDLES
HE CALLED HIMSELF A "CLEANER".
ILL NIÑO
AND HE SHOT OUR FRIEND.

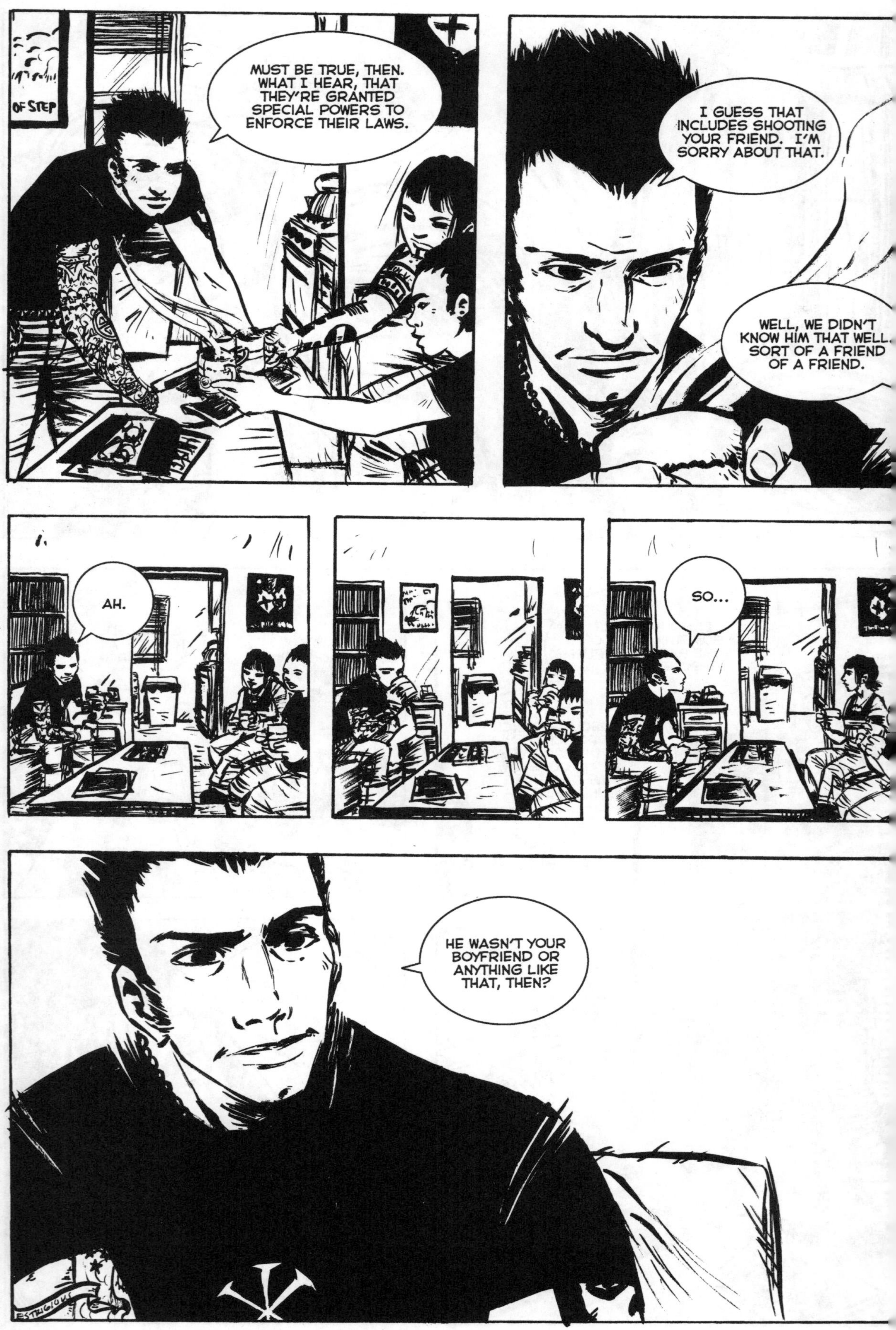
MUST BE TRUE, THEN. WHAT I HEAR, THAT THEY'RE GRANTED SPECIAL POWERS TO ENFORCE THEIR LAWS.
I GUESS THAT INCLUDES SHOOTING YOUR FRIEND. I'M SORRY ABOUT THAT.
WELL, WE DIDN'T KNOW HIM THAT WELL. SORT OF A FRIEND OF A FRIEND.
AH.
SO...
HE WASN'T YOUR BOYFRIEND OR ANYTHING LIKE THAT, THEN?

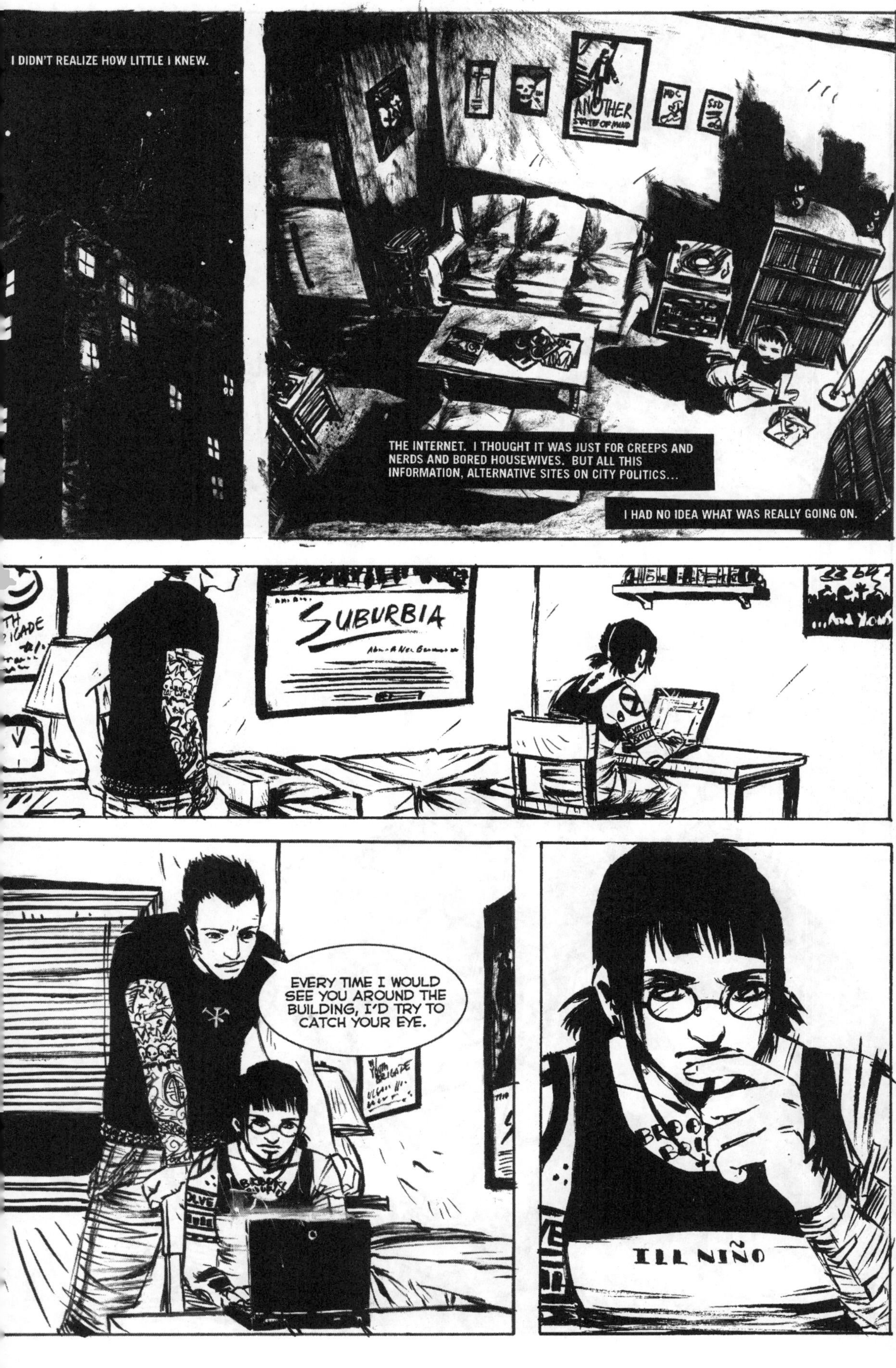
I DIDN'T REALIZE HOW LITTLE I KNEW.
ANOTHER
STATE OF MIND
MDC
SSD
THE INTERNET. I THOUGHT IT WAS JUST FOR CREEPS AND NERDS AND BORED HOUSEWIVES. BUT ALL THIS INFORMATION, ALTERNATIVE SITES ON CITY POLITICS...
I HAD NO IDEA WHAT WAS REALLY GOING ON.
SUBURBIA
EVERY TIME I WOULD SEE YOU AROUND THE BUILDING, I'D TRY TO CATCH YOUR EYE.
ILL NIÑO

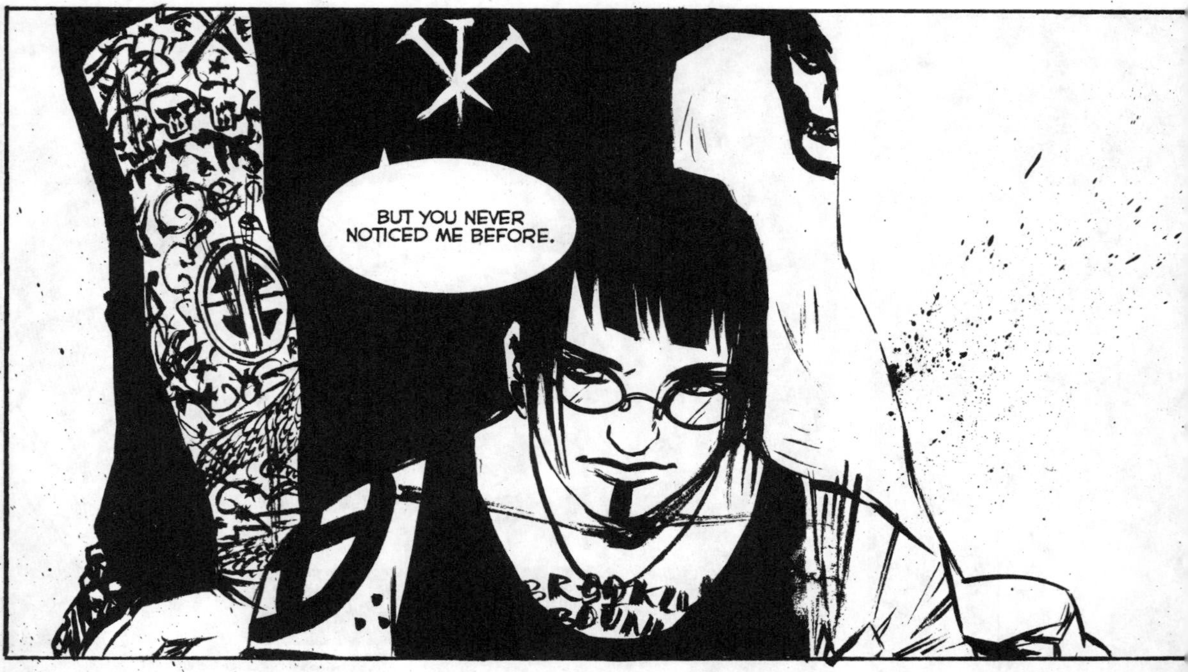
BUT YOU NEVER NOTICED ME BEFORE.
BROOKLYN BOUND

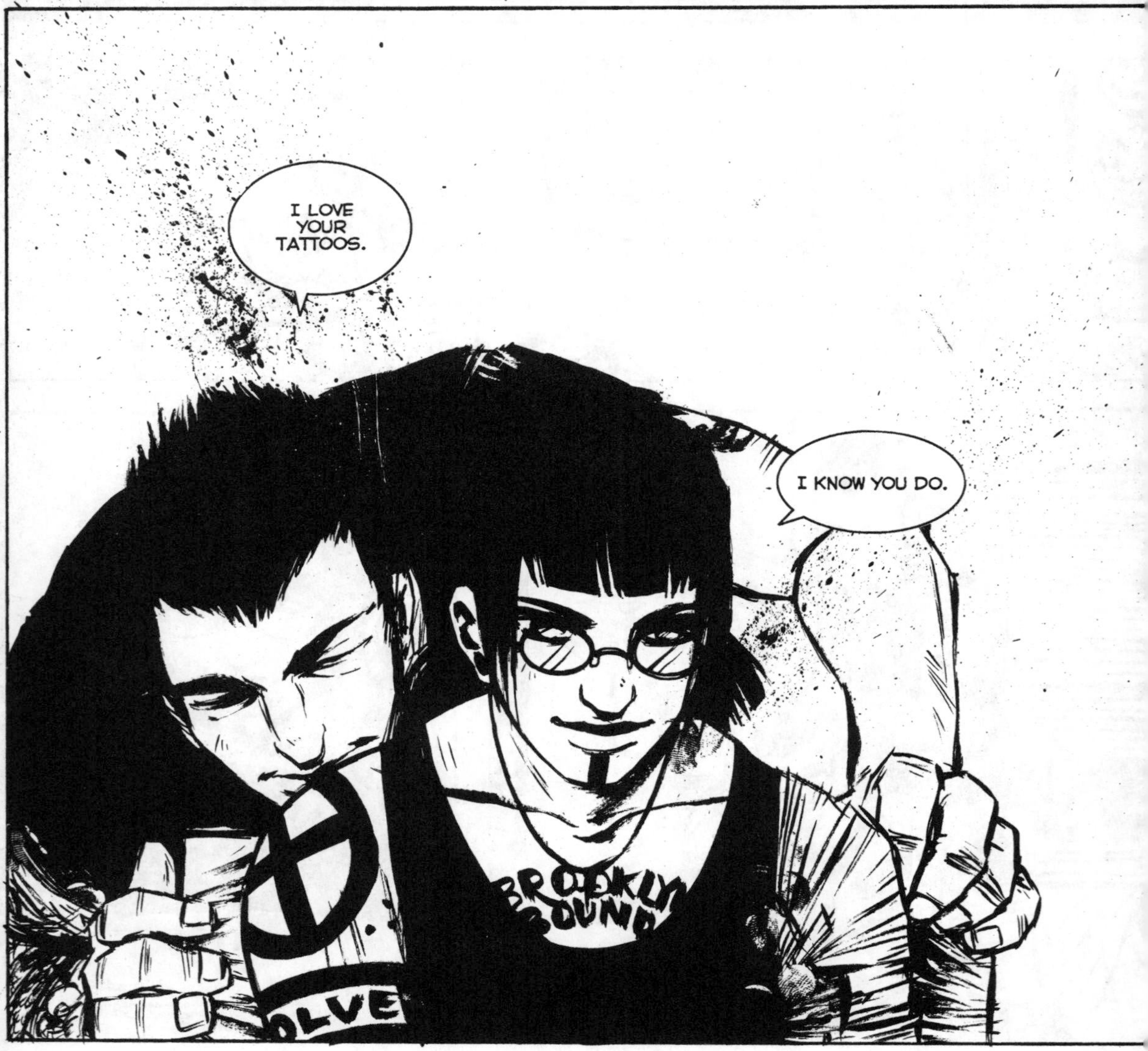
I LOVE YOUR TATTOOS.
I KNOW YOU DO.
BROOKLYN BOUND
OLVE

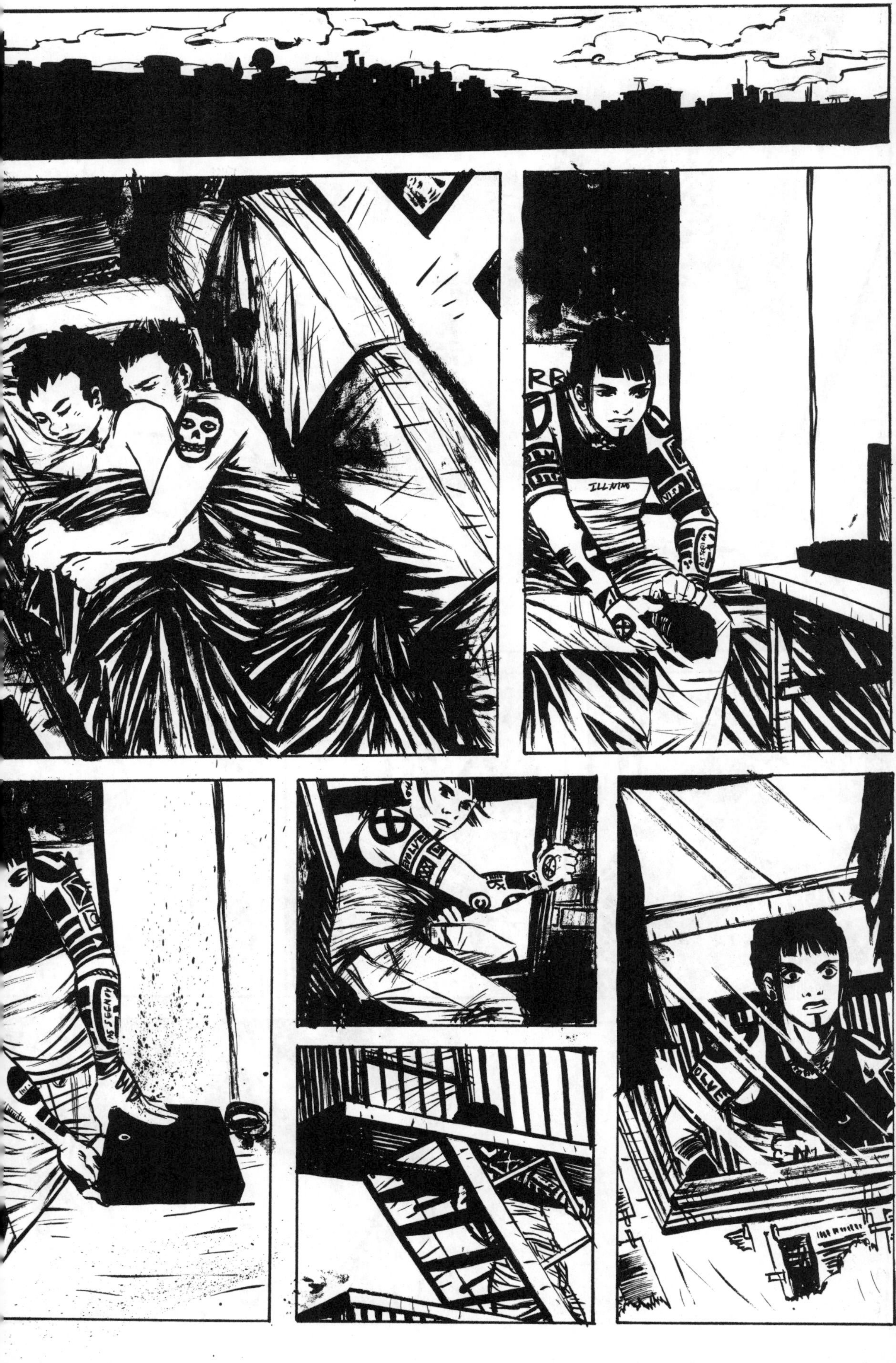

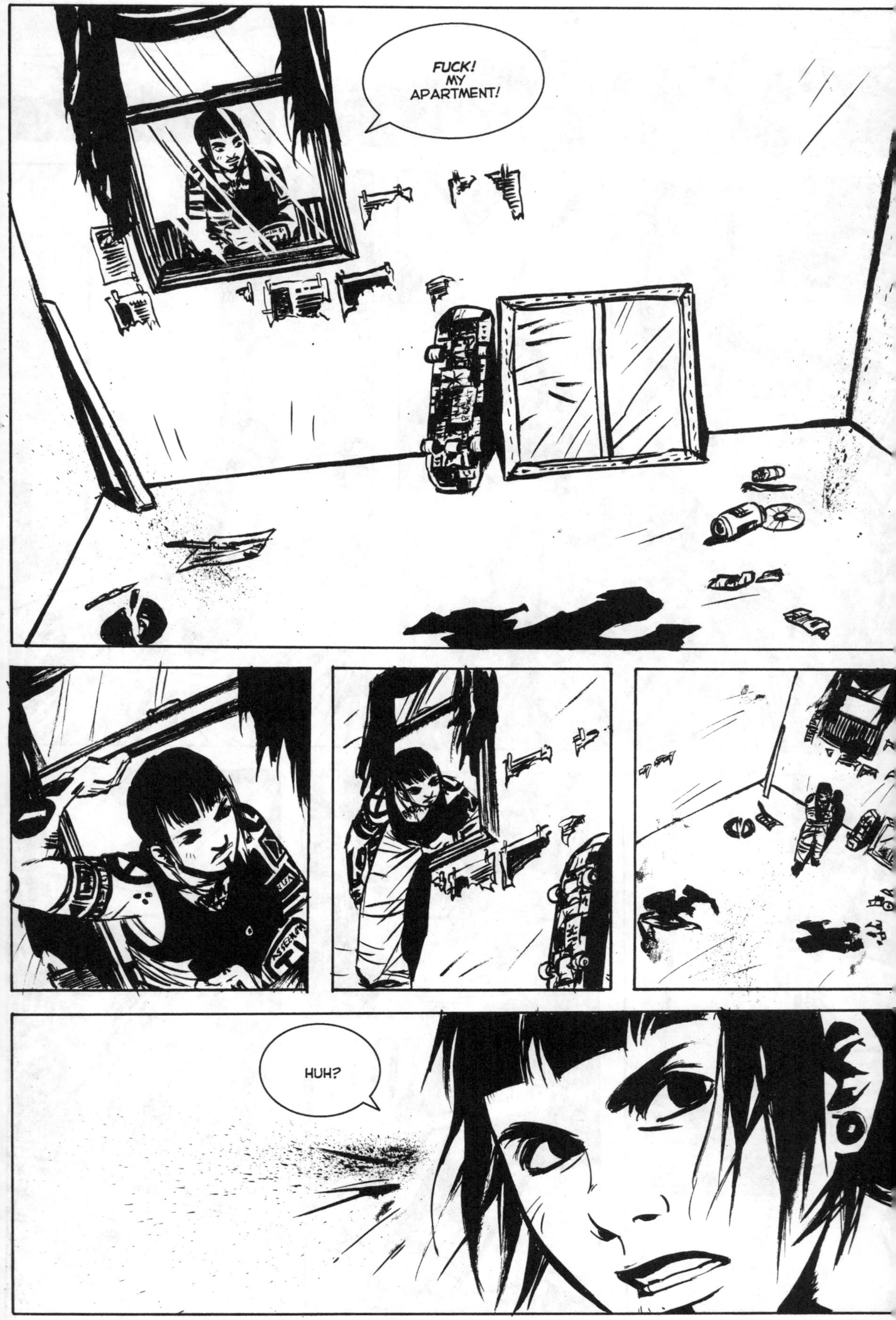
FUCK! MY APARTMENT!
HUH?

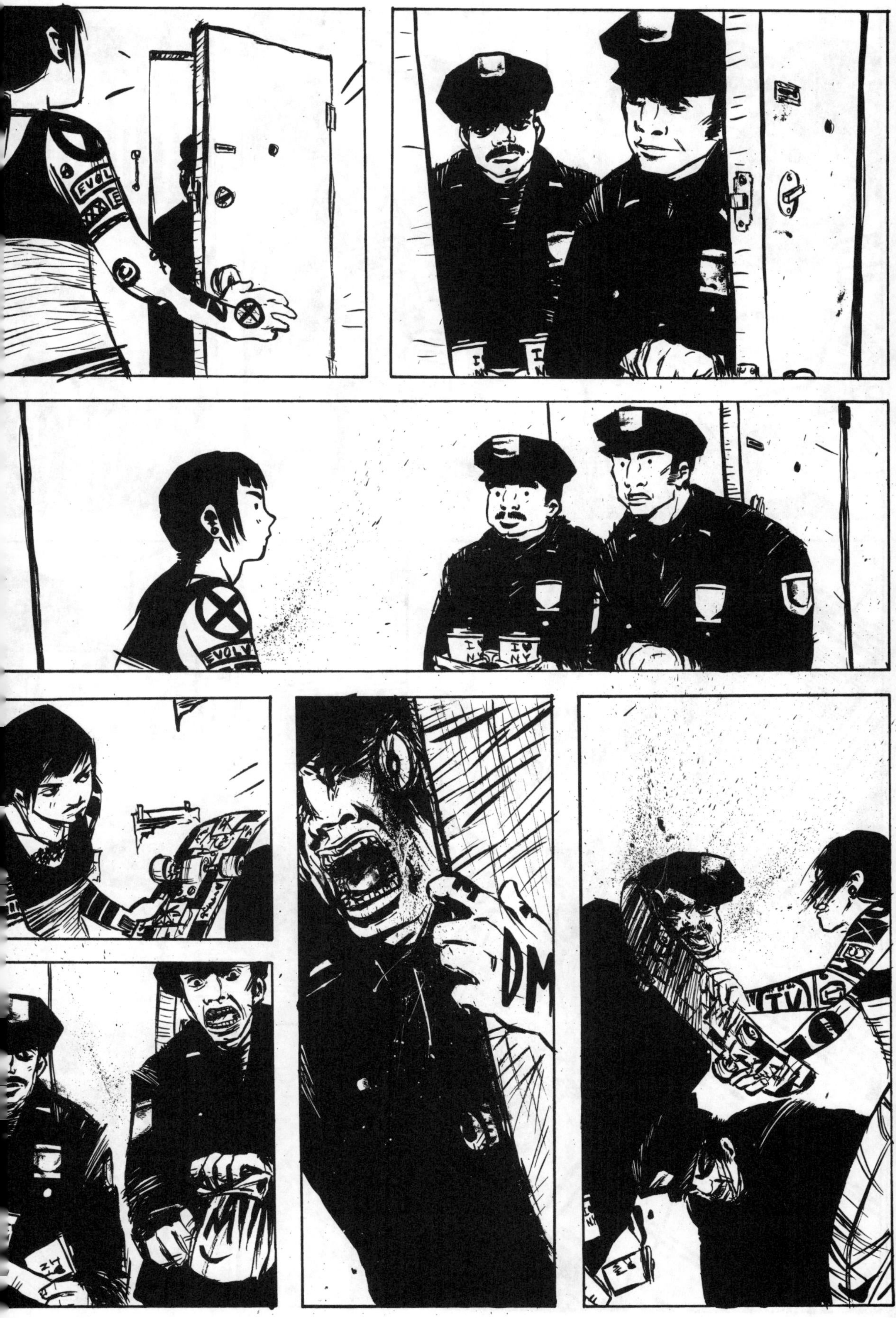
DM

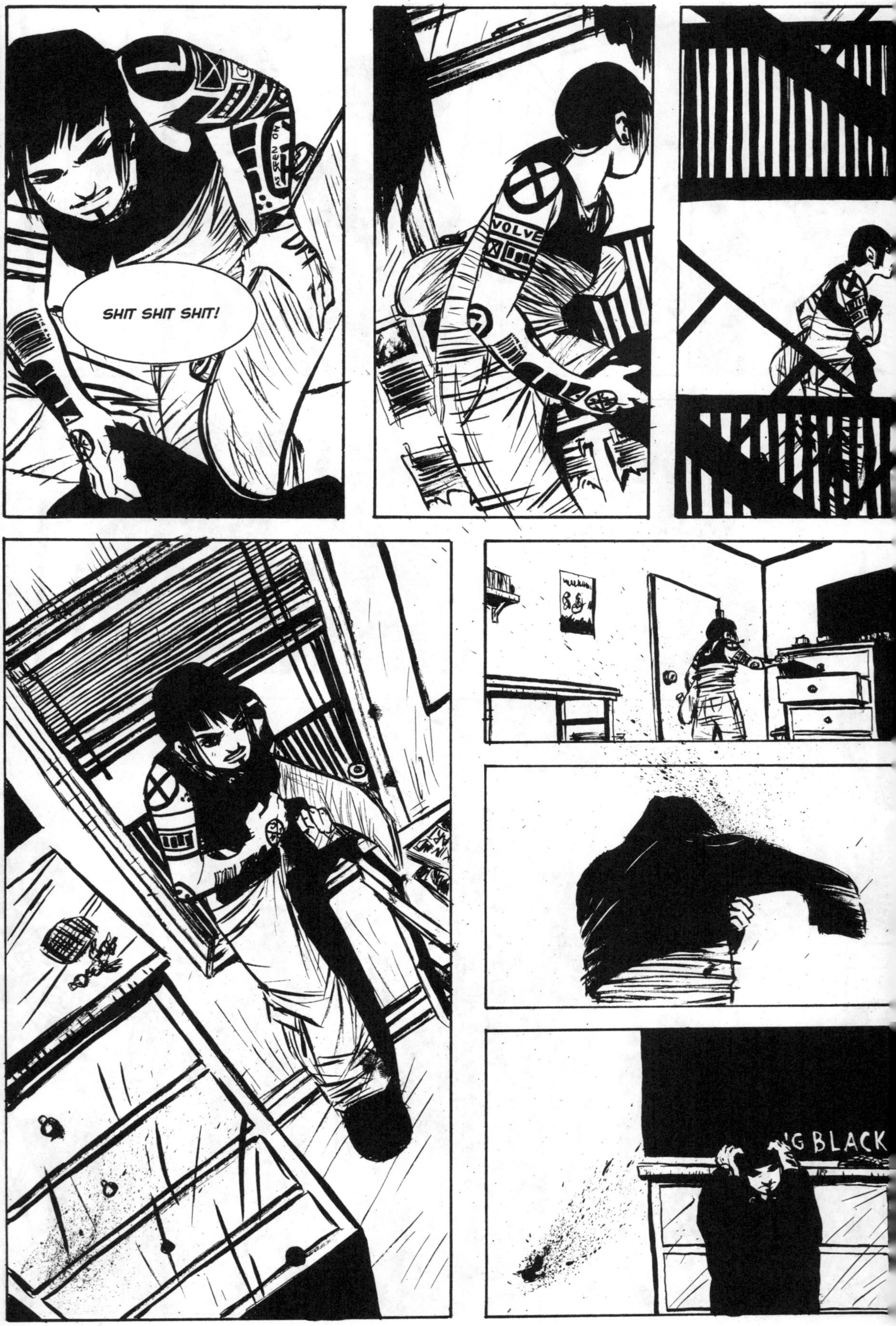
SHIT SHIT SHIT!
AS SEEN ON
VOLVE
G BLACK

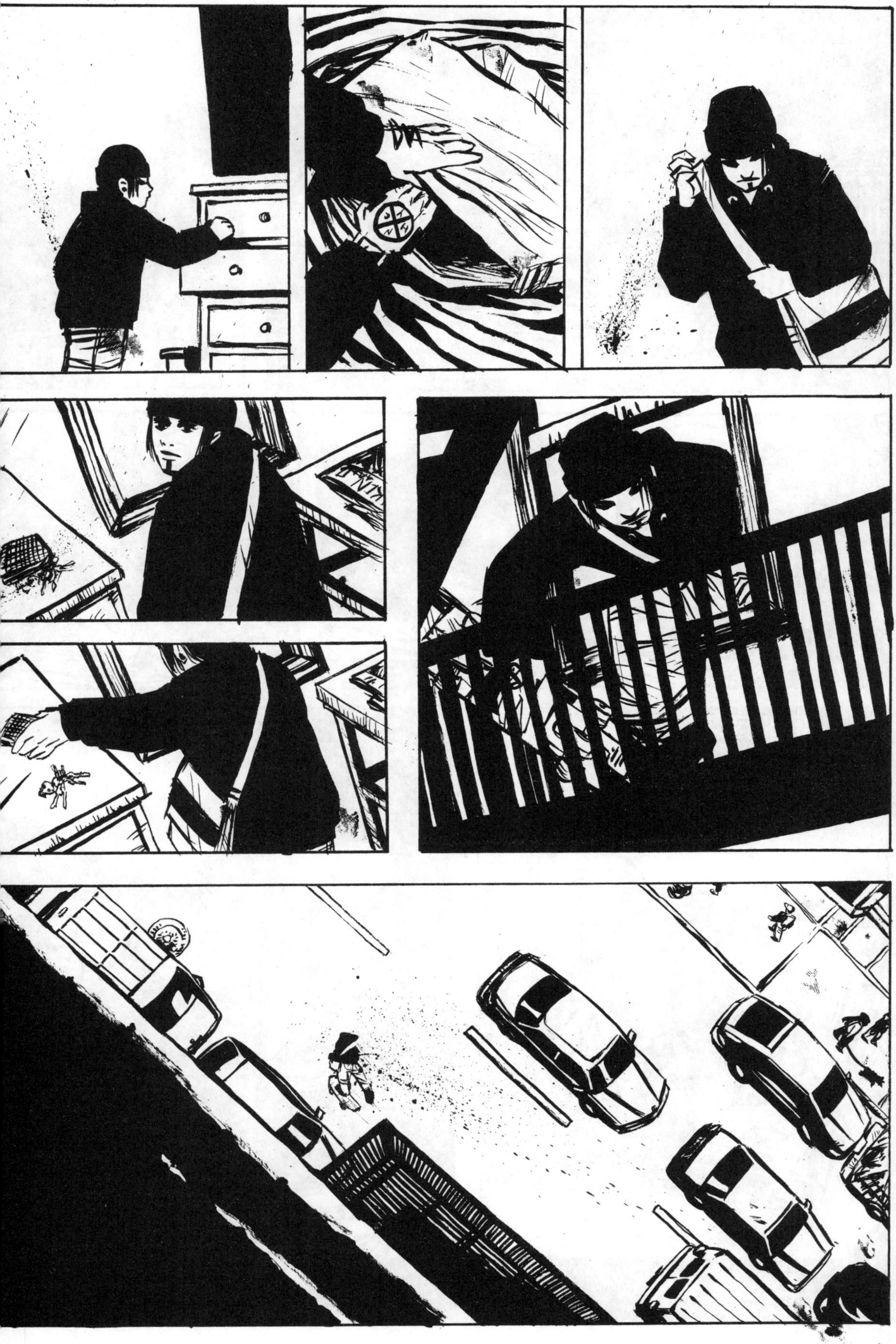

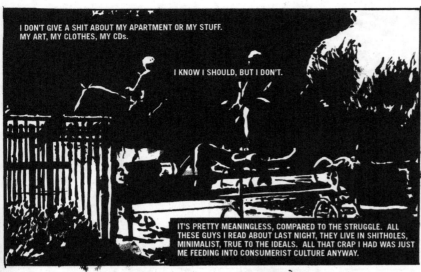

I DON'T GIVE A SHIT ABOUT MY APARTMENT OR MY STUFF. MY ART, MY CLOTHES, MY CDS.

I KNOW I SHOULD, BUT I DON'T.

IT'S PRETTY MEANINGLESS, COMPARED TO THE STRUGGLE. ALL THESE GUYS I READ ABOUT LAST NIGHT, THEY LIVE IN SHITHOLES, MINIMALIST, TRUE TO THE IDEALS. ALL THAT CRAP I HAD WAS JUST ME FEEDING INTO CONSUMERIST CULTURE ANYWAY.

HOLY SHIT.

IF I'M GONNA BE AN EFFECTIVE FIGHTER IN THIS WAR, I'M GONNA HAVE TO LEARN TO CAST OFF THE DEAD WEIGHT OF THIS CULTURE. LIVE OFF THE CITY AND THE MOVEMENT THE WAY GUERILLA FIGHTERS LIVE OFF THE LAND, THEY WAY THEY USE IT TO THEIR ADVANTAGE.

PEOPLE LIKE KURT, WITH HIS MUSIC AND MONEY AND BULLSHIT, ARE THE SYMBOL OF WHAT'S WRONG. MINDLESSLY FOLLOWING TRENDS, IMMERSING HIMSELF IN A SICK CULTURE, YET STILL THINKING HE'S FRINGE, HE'S HARDCORE.

FUCKING ASSHOLE.

PLUS, THE THOUGHT OF THAT GUY CREEPING OUT ON ME FOR GOD KNOWS HOW LONG IS ENOUGH TO MAKE ME NOT FEEL BAD FOR RIPPING HIM OFF.

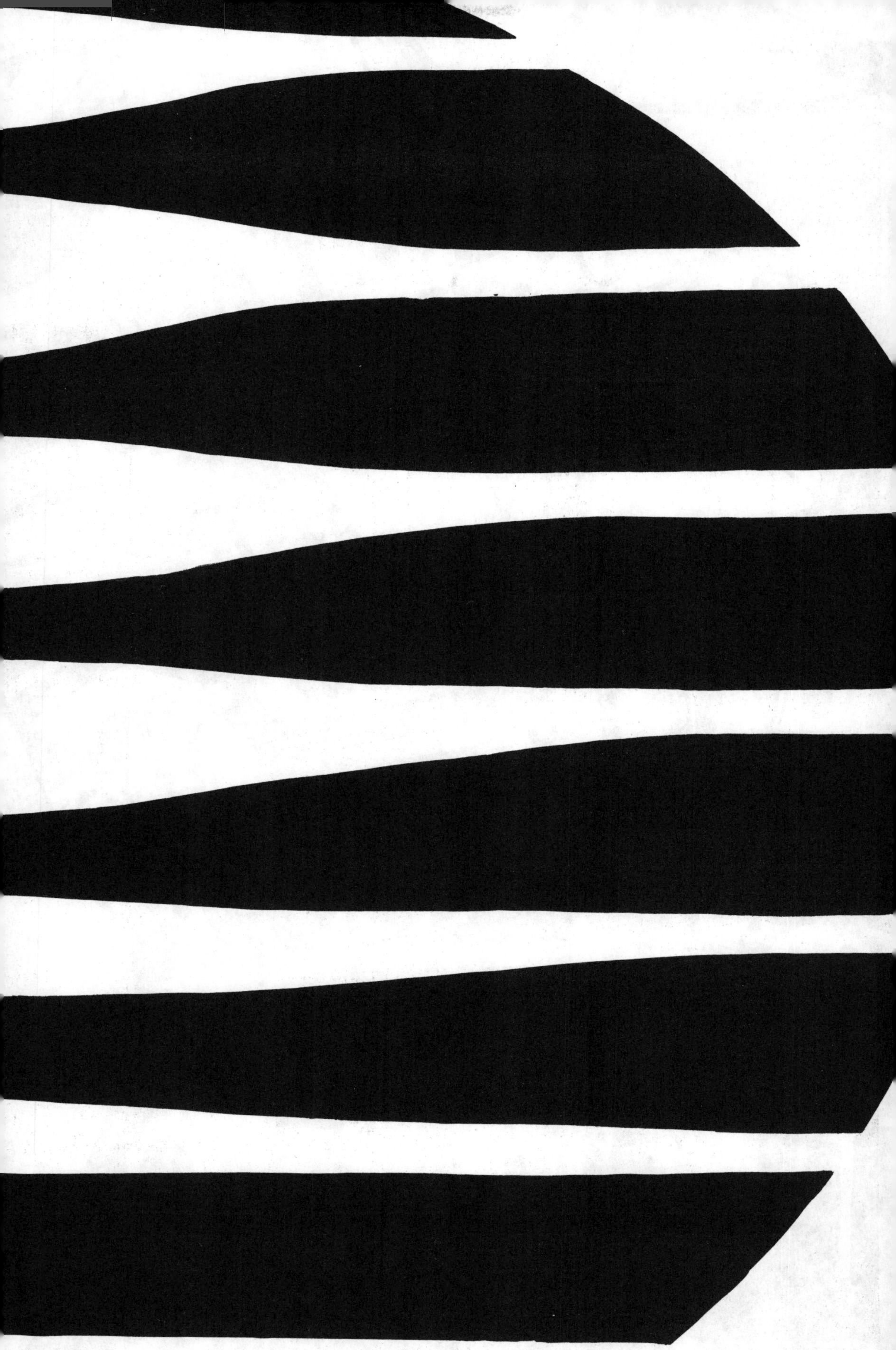

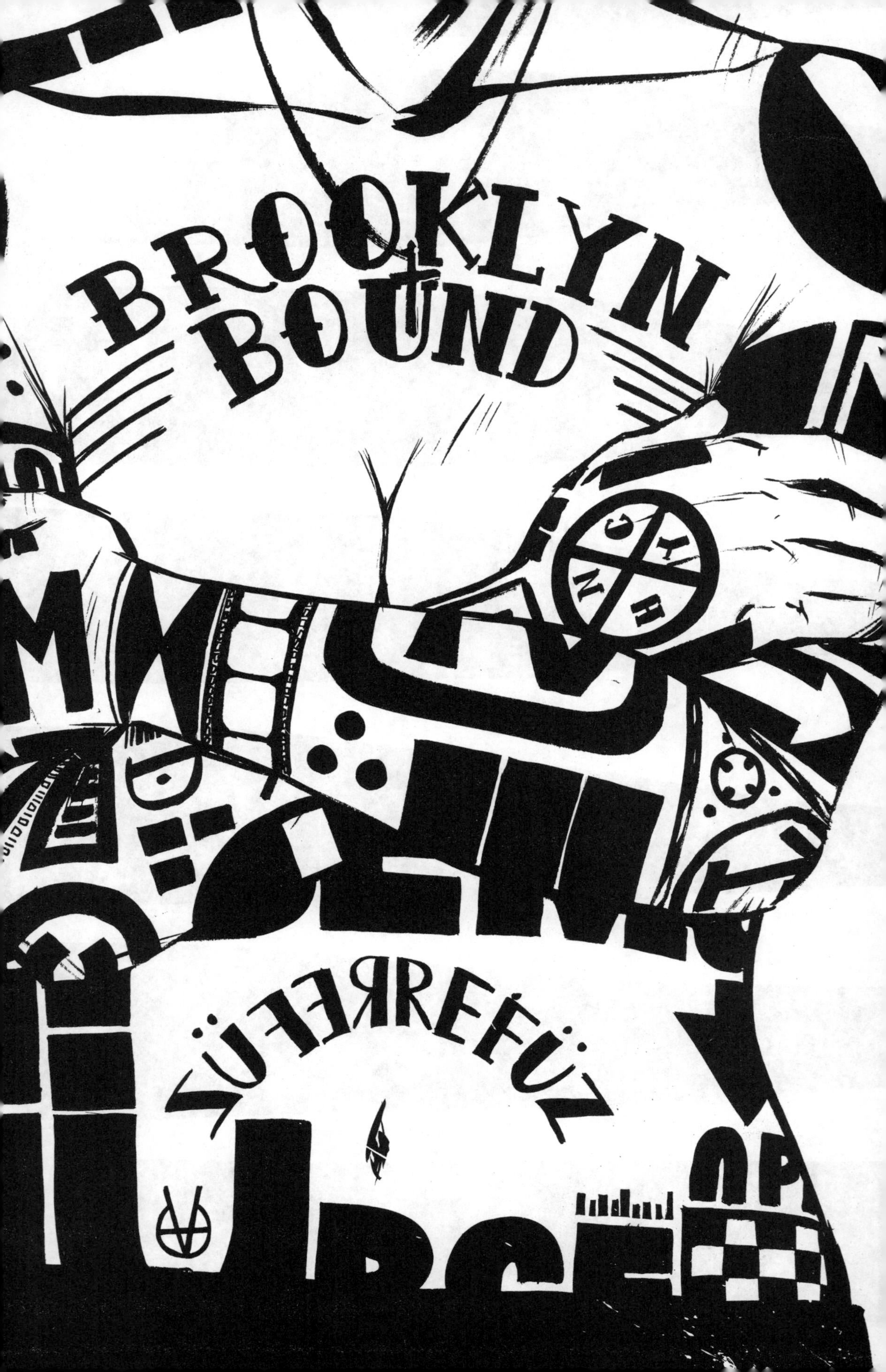
BROOKLYN BOUND
SÜFFERREFÜZ

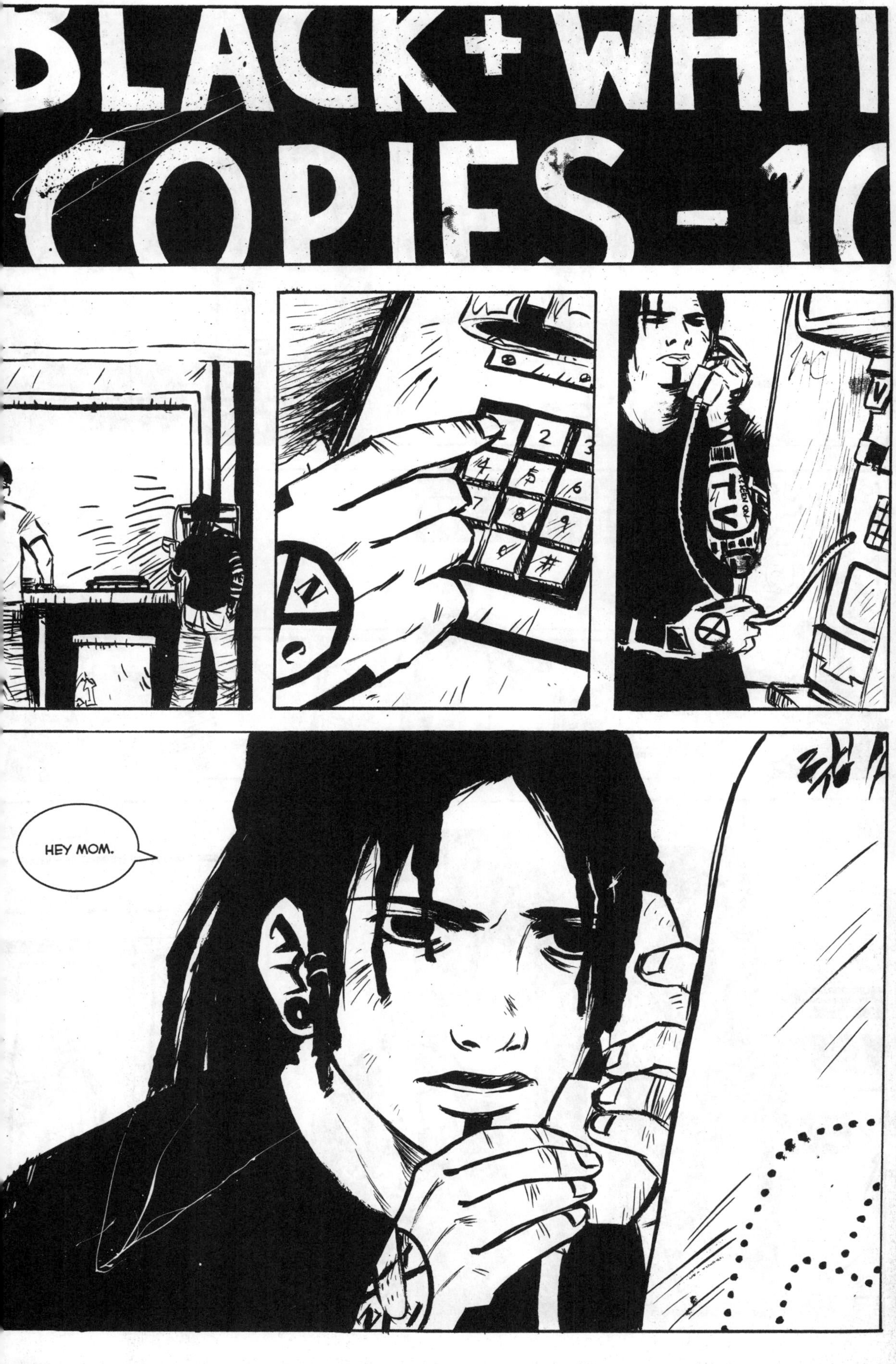
BLACK+WHI
COPIES-10
TV
HEY MOM.

MY MOM.

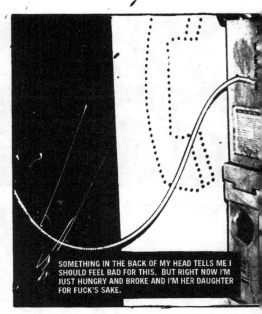

SOMETHING IN THE BACK OF MY HEAD TELLS ME I SHOULD FEEL BAD FOR THIS. BUT RIGHT NOW I'M JUST HUNGRY AND BROKE AND I'M HER DAUGHTER FOR FUCK'S SAKE.

SHE'S PISSED BECAUSE I DROPPED OUT OF SCHOOL AND DIDN'T TELL HER AND HARDLY CALL NOW. WELL, THE SCHOOL WAS BULLSHIT. I WAS WASTING HER MONEY. SHE DISAGREES.

PRINTS ONLY $12⁹⁹

shit.

SHE'S FUCKING IMPOSSIBLE TO DEAL WITH RIGHT NOW.

AND NO, SHE ISN'T GONNA GIVE ME ANY MONEY. NOT UNTIL I COME HOME AND "EXPLAIN MYSELF", SHE SAYS.

FUCK THAT.

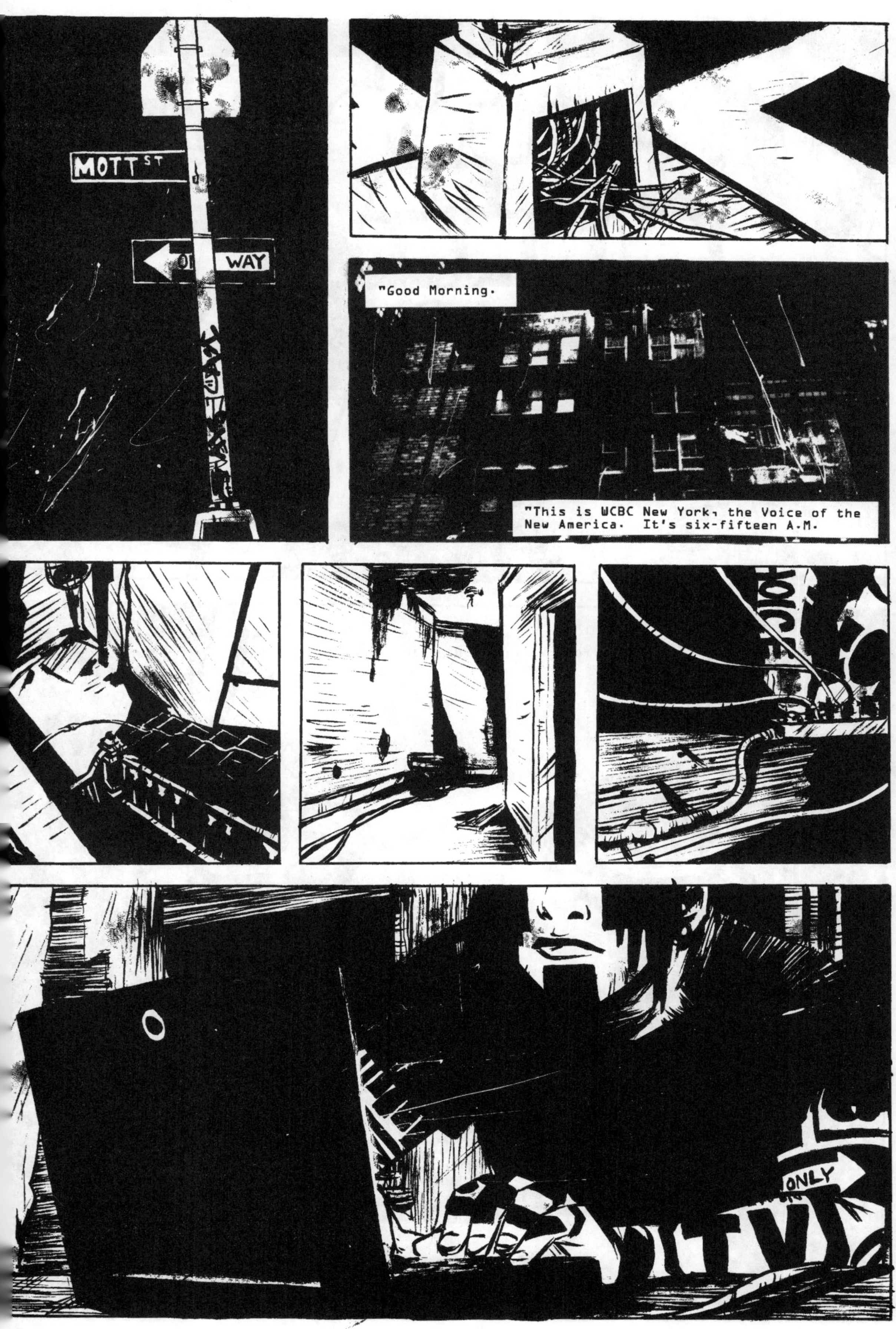

MOTT ST
WAY
"Good Morning.
"This is WCBC New York, the Voice of the New America. It's six-fifteen A.M.
ONLY

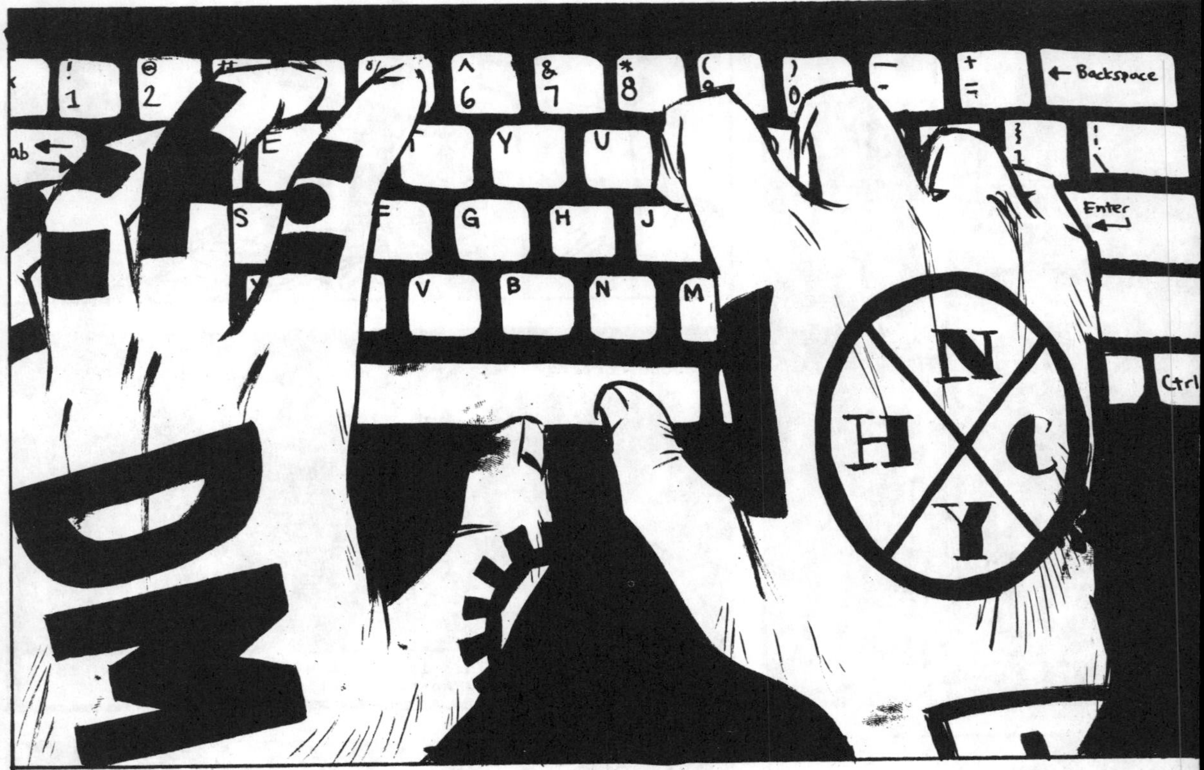
Backspace
Enter
Ctrl

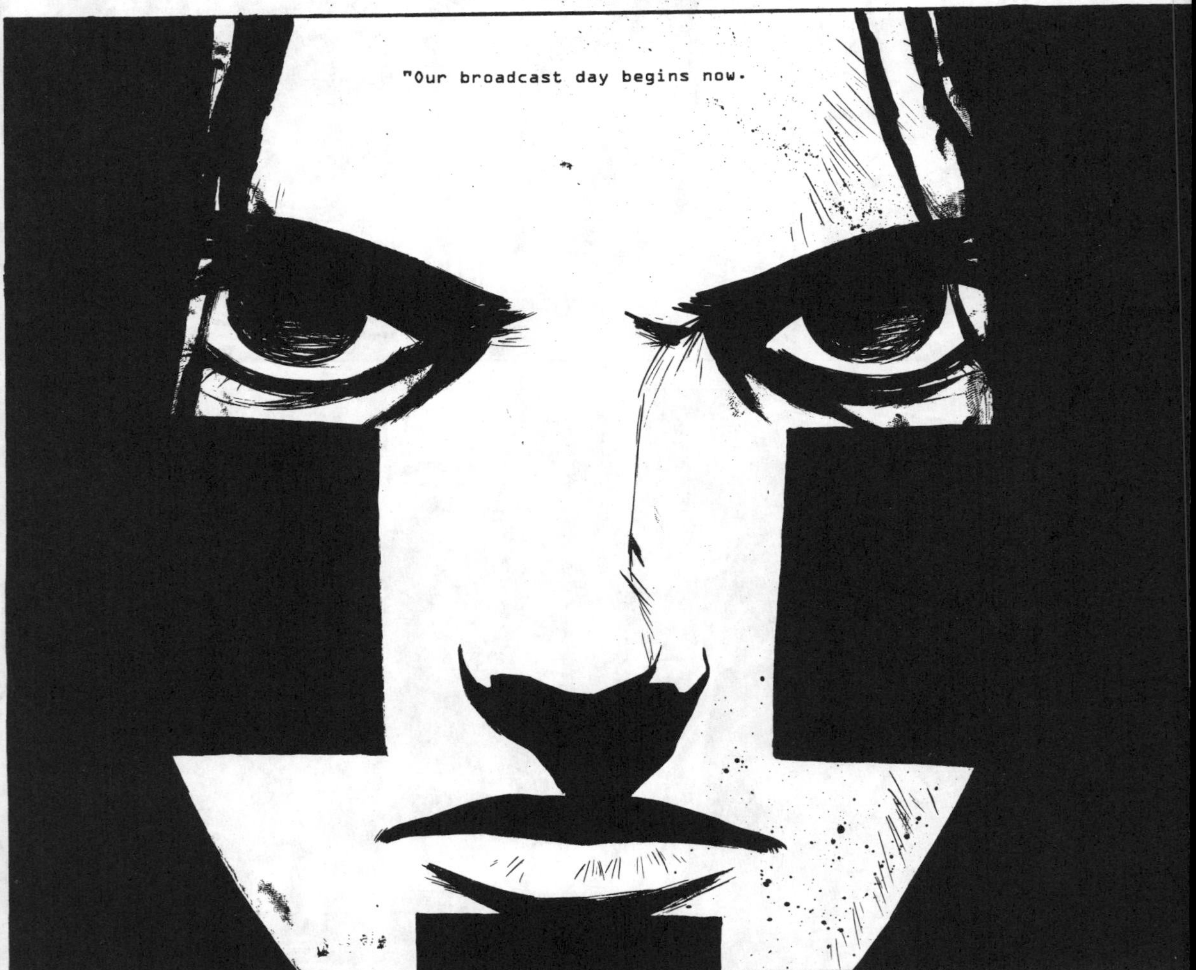
"Our broadcast day begins now.

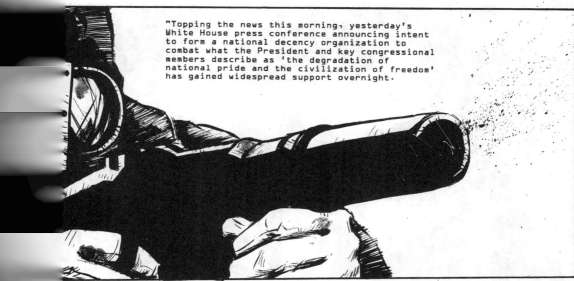

"Topping the news this morning, yesterday's White House press conference announcing intent to form a national decency organization to combat what the President and key congressional members describe as 'the degradation of national pride and the civilization of freedom' has gained widespread support overnight.

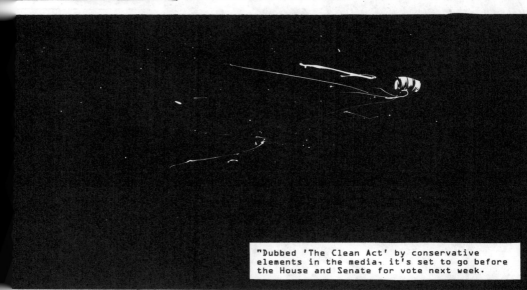

"Dubbed 'The Clean Act' by conservative elements in the media, it's set to go before the House and Senate for vote next week.

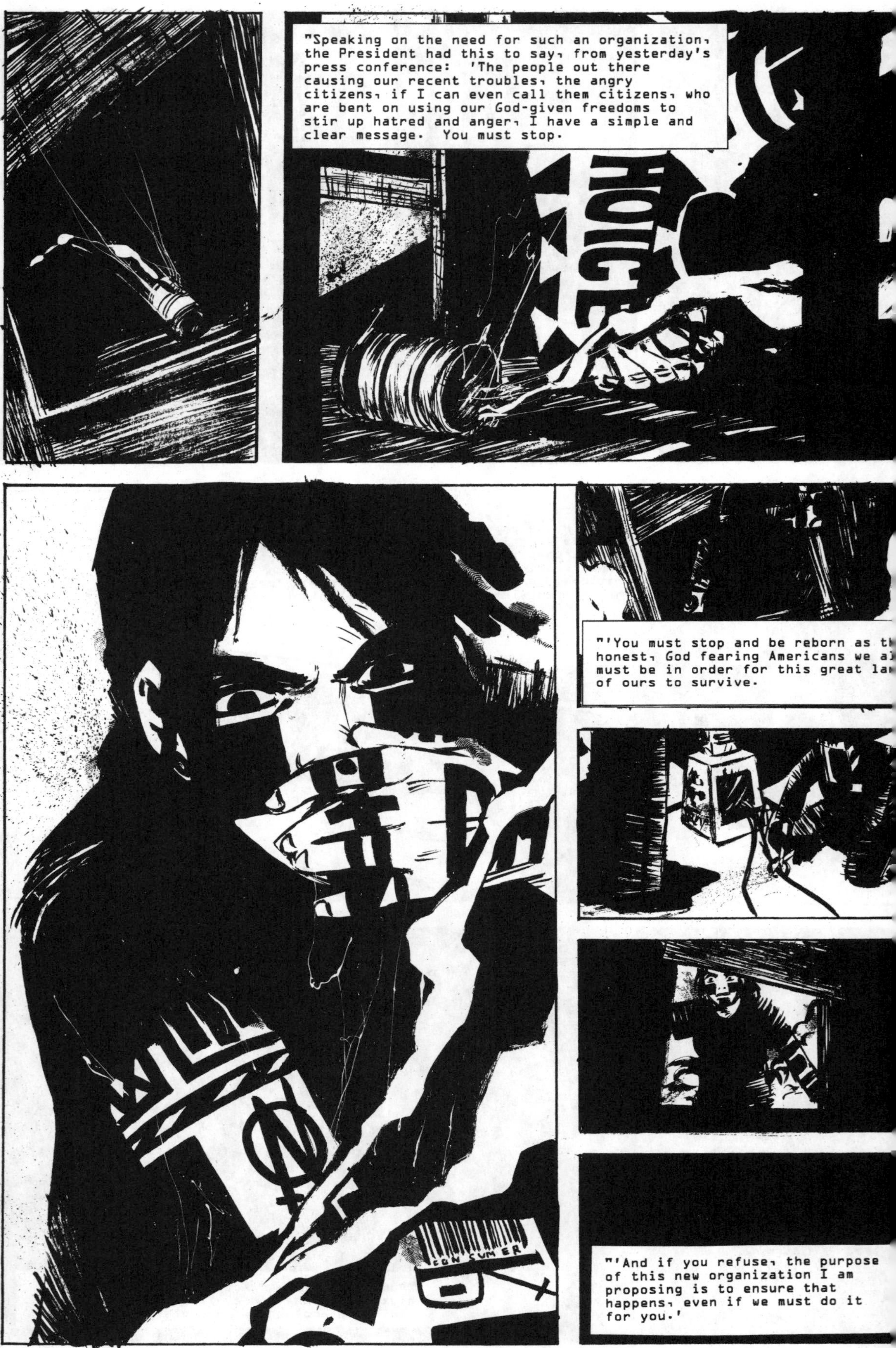
"Speaking on the need for such an organization, the President had this to say, from yesterday's press conference: 'The people out there causing our recent troubles, the angry citizens, if I can even call them citizens, who are bent on using our God-given freedoms to stir up hatred and anger, I have a simple and clear message. You must stop.
"'You must stop and be reborn as t honest, God fearing Americans we a must be in order for this great la of ours to survive.
"'And if you refuse, the purpose of this new organization I am proposing is to ensure that happens, even if we must do it for you.'
CONSUMER

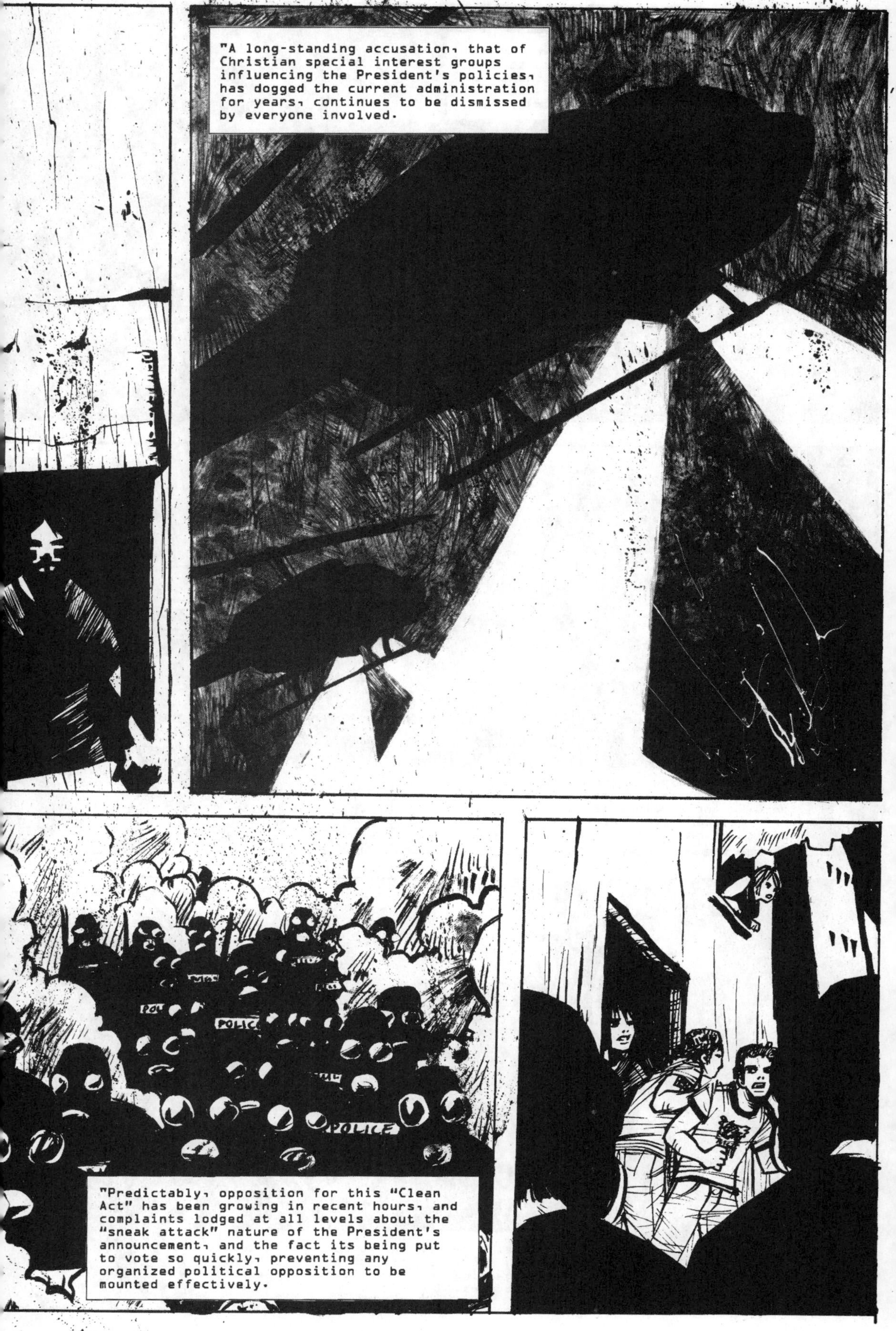
"A long-standing accusation, that of Christian special interest groups influencing the President's policies, has dogged the current administration for years, continues to be dismissed by everyone involved.
POLICE
POLICE
"Predictably, opposition for this "Clean Act" has been growing in recent hours, and complaints lodged at all levels about the "sneak attack" nature of the President's announcement, and the fact its being put to vote so quickly, preventing any organized political opposition to be mounted effectively.

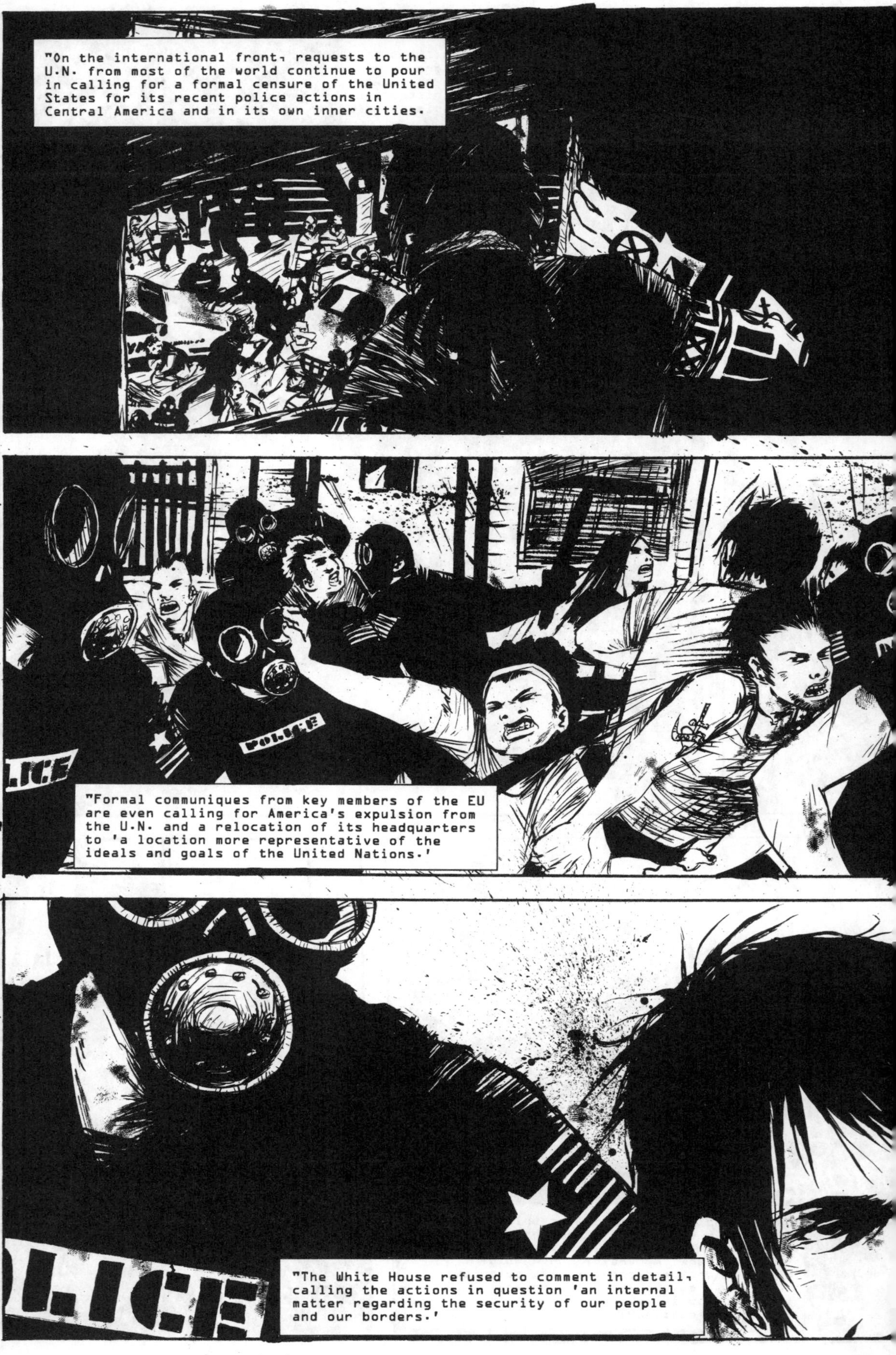
"On the international front, requests to the U.N. from most of the world continue to pour in calling for a formal censure of the United States for its recent police actions in Central America and in its own inner cities.
POLICE
LICE
"Formal communiques from key members of the EU are even calling for America's expulsion from the U.N. and a relocation of its headquarters to 'a location more representative of the ideals and goals of the United Nations.'
LICE
"The White House refused to comment in detail, calling the actions in question 'an internal matter regarding the security of our people and our borders.'

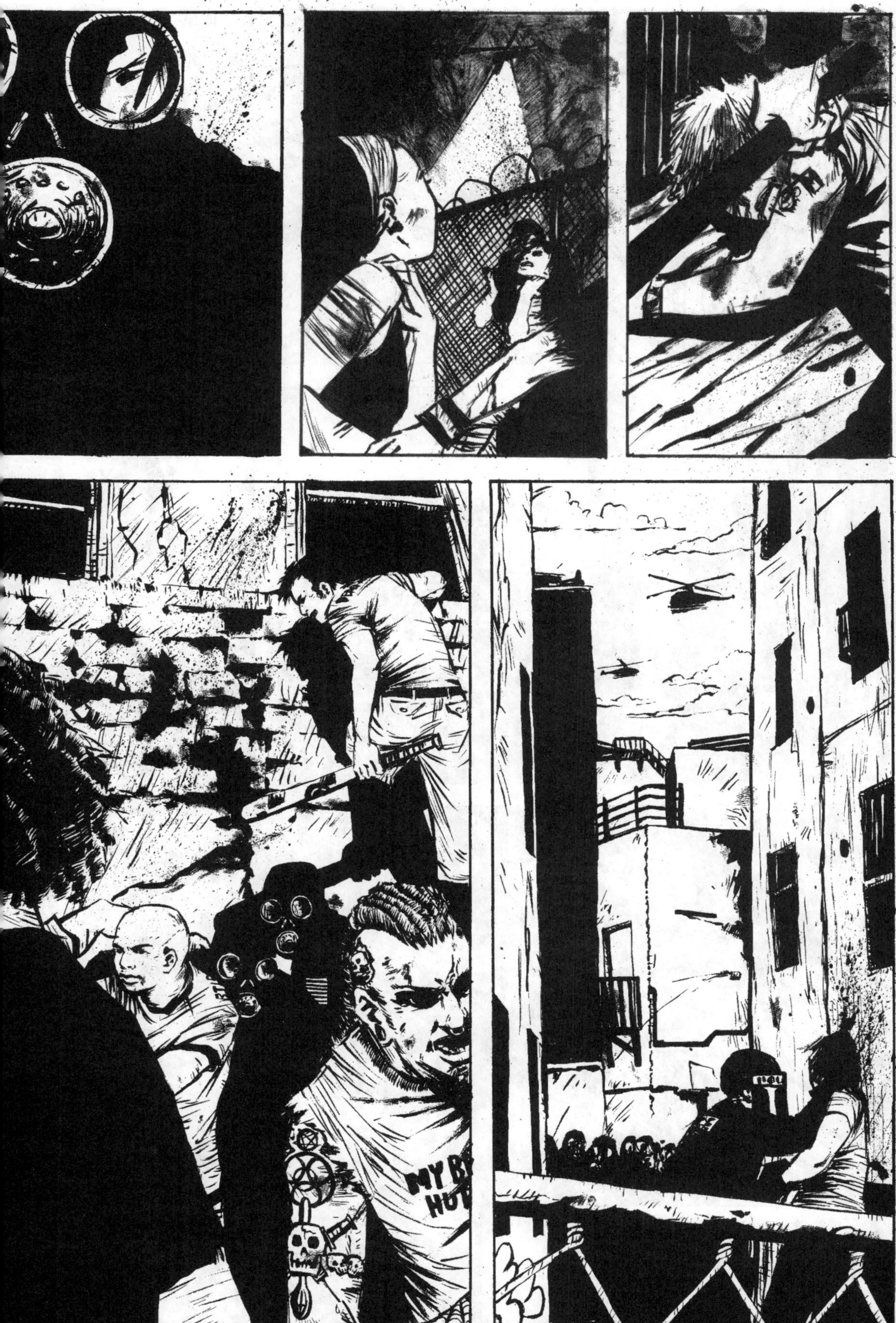

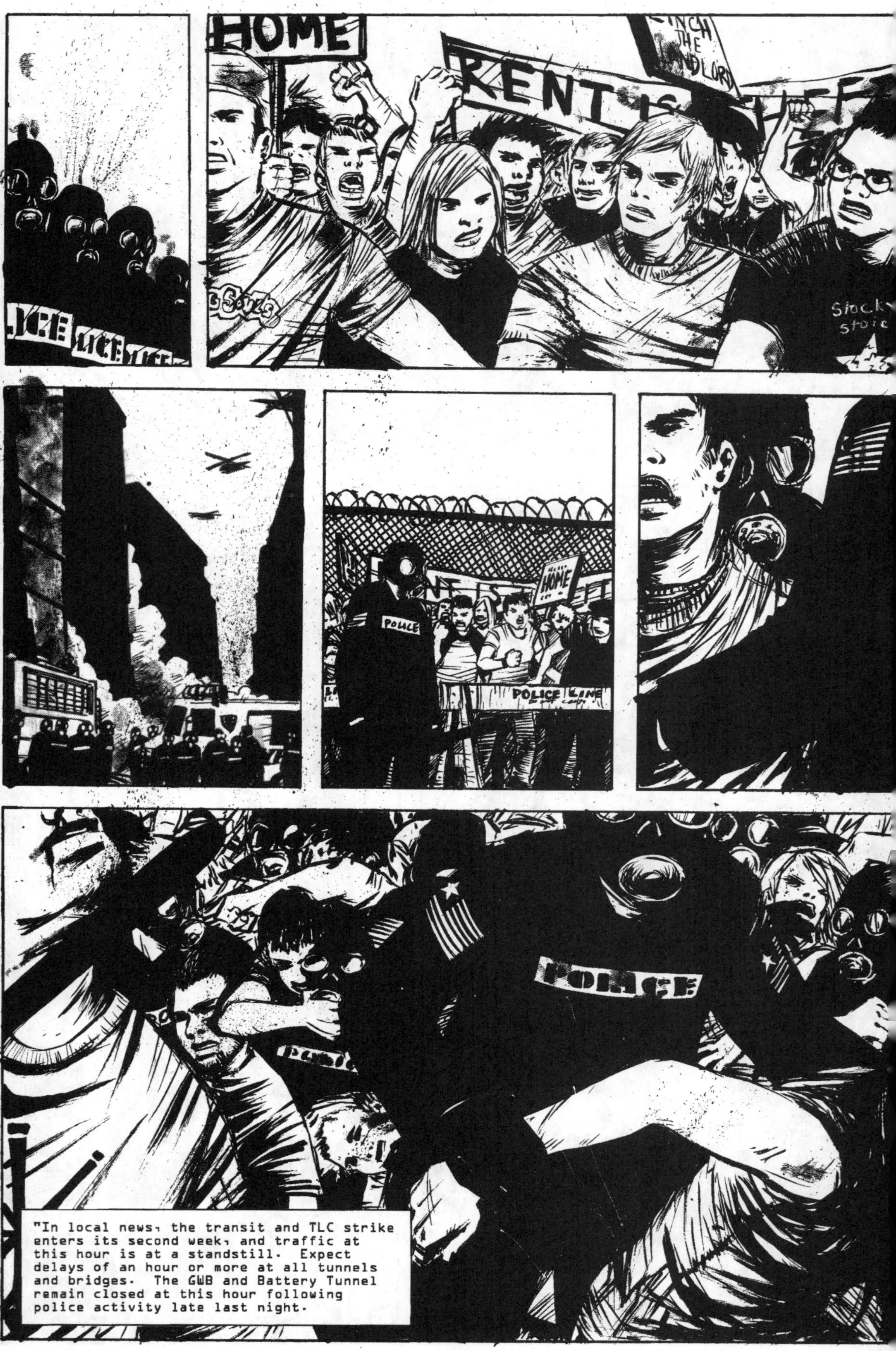
HOME
POLICE
POLICE LINE
POLICE
"In local news, the transit and TLC strike enters its second week, and traffic at this hour is at a standstill. Expect delays of an hour or more at all tunnels and bridges. The GWB and Battery Tunnel remain closed at this hour following police activity late last night.

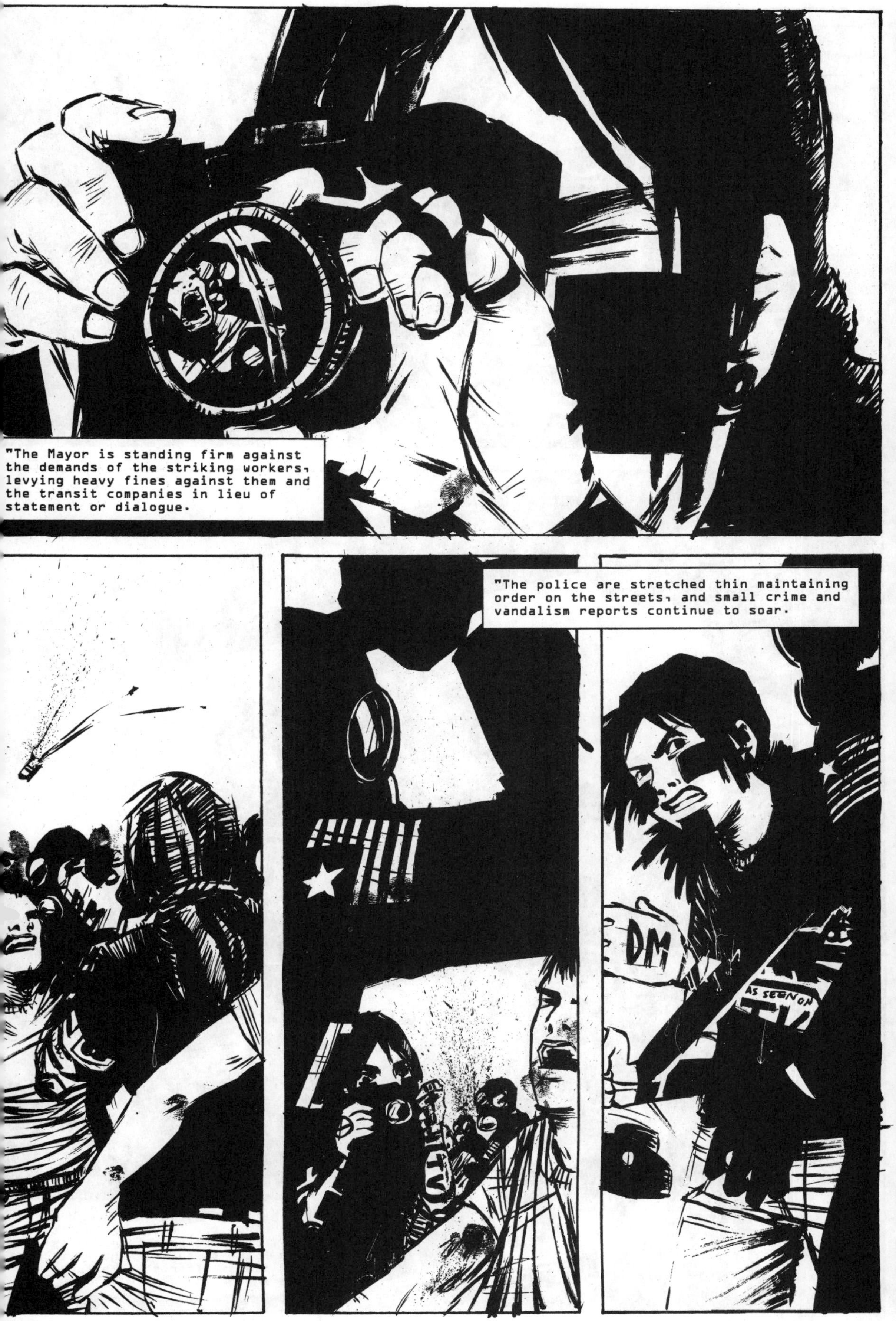
"The Mayor is standing firm against the demands of the striking workers, levying heavy fines against them and the transit companies in lieu of statement or dialogue.
"The police are stretched thin maintaining order on the streets, and small crime and vandalism reports continue to soar.
TV
DM
AS SEEN ON

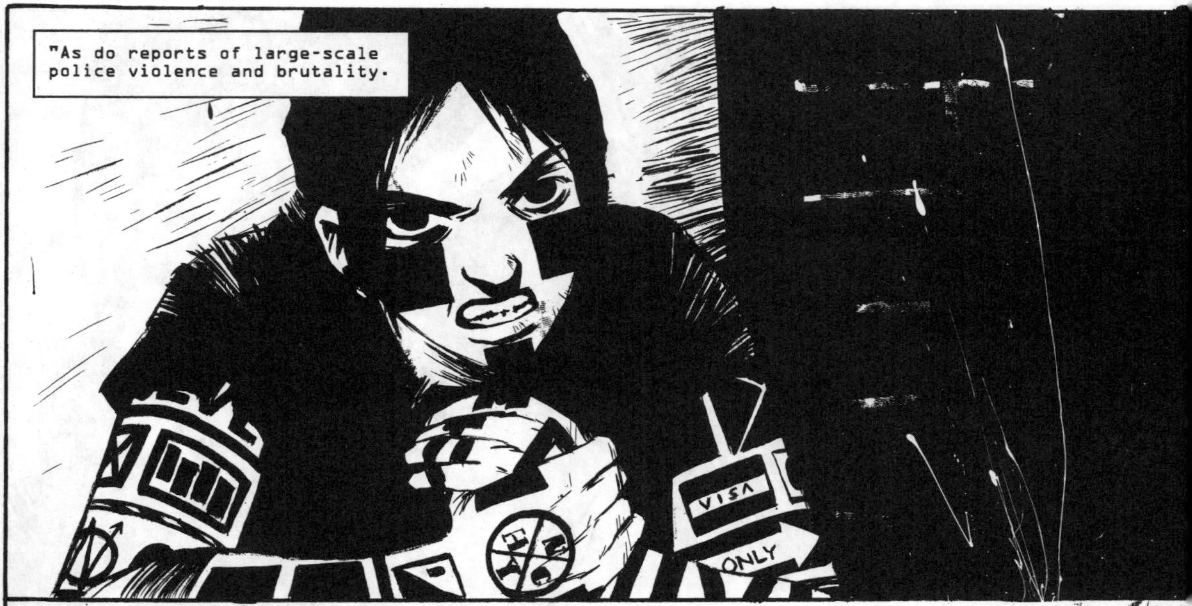
"As do reports of large-scale police violence and brutality.
VISA
ONLY

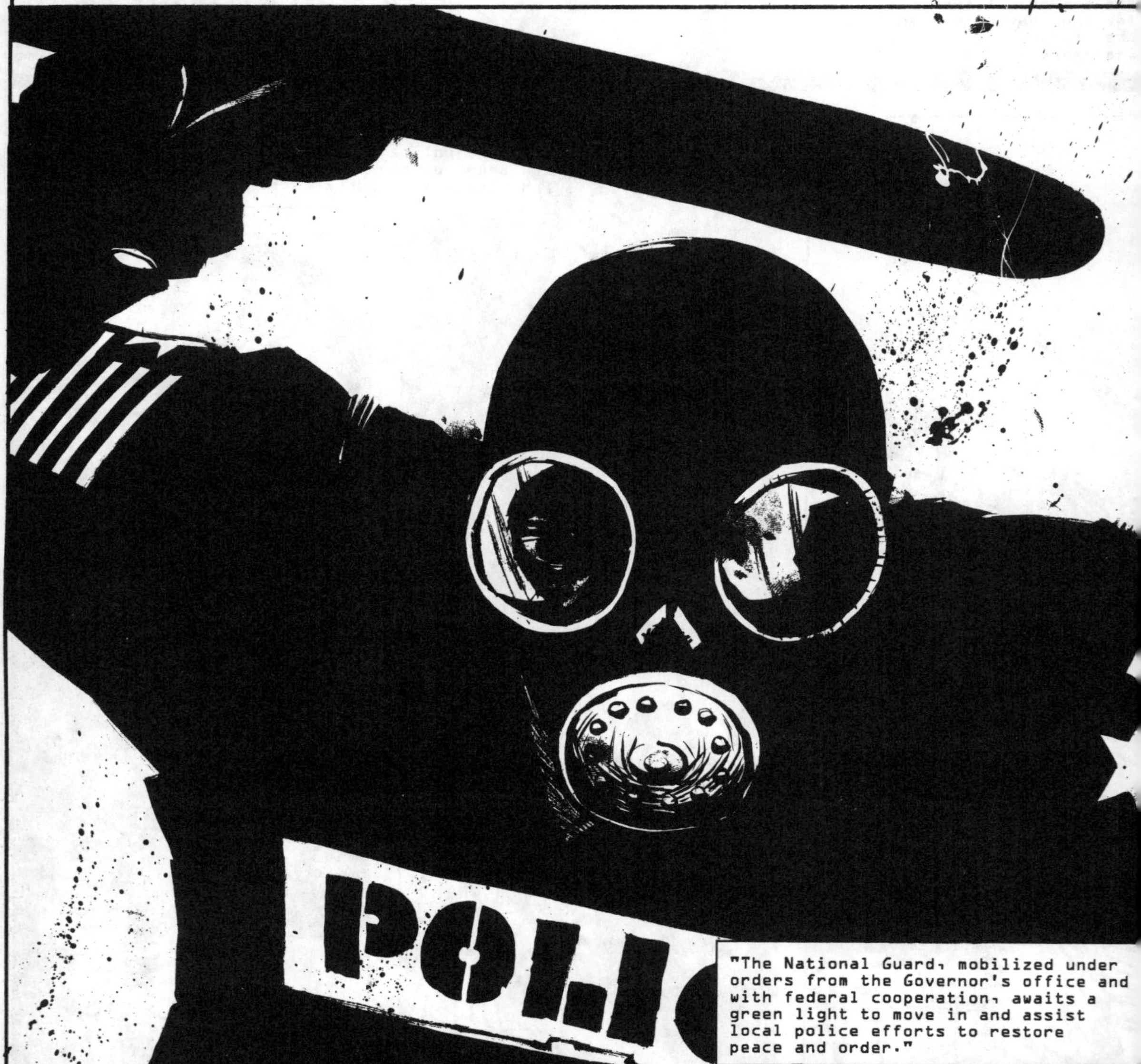
POLIC
"The National Guard, mobilized under orders from the Governor's office and with federal cooperation, awaits a green light to move in and assist local police efforts to restore peace and order."

THAT'S WHEN IT ALL CHANGED.

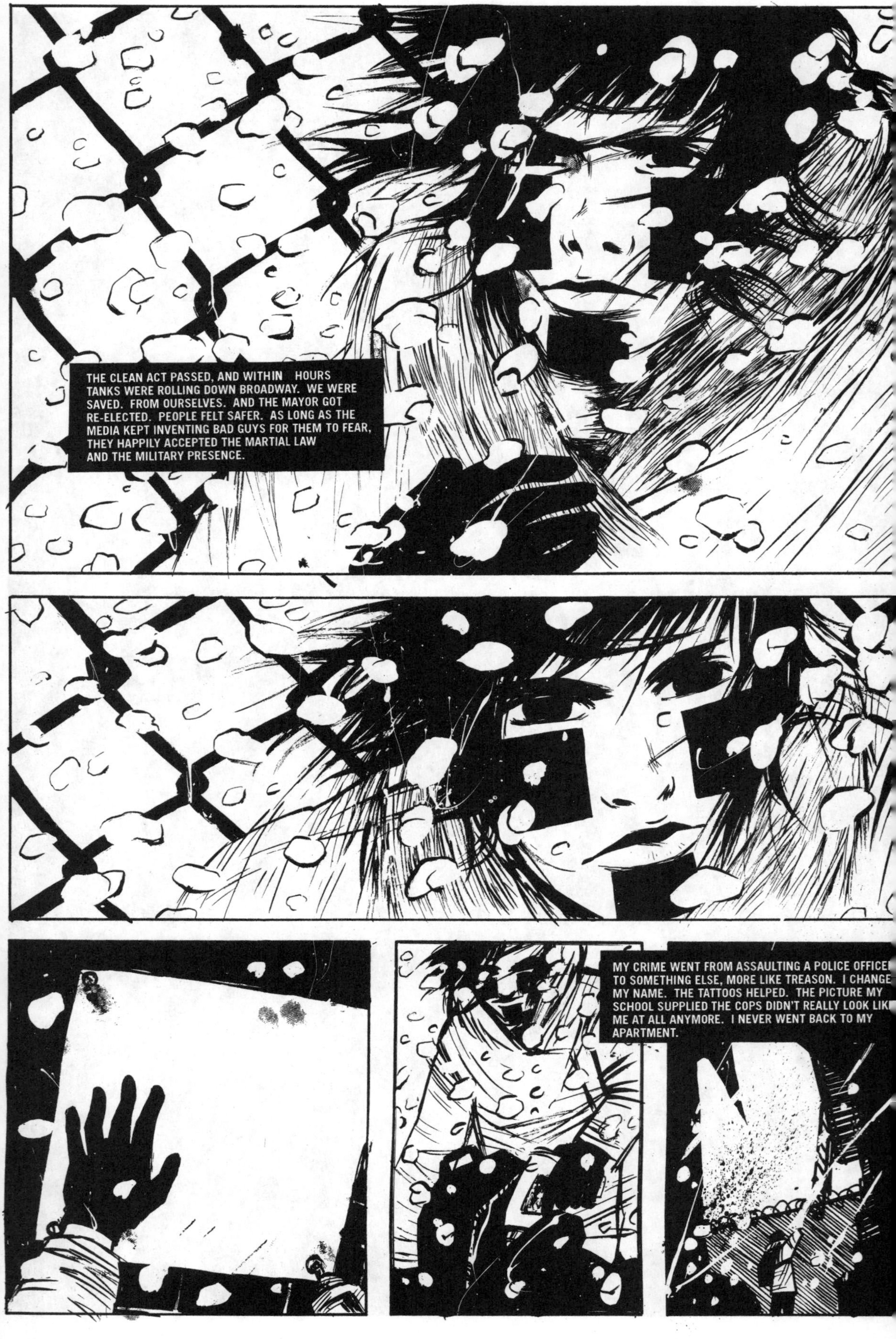
THE CLEAN ACT PASSED, AND WITHIN HOURS TANKS WERE ROLLING DOWN BROADWAY. WE WERE SAVED. FROM OURSELVES. AND THE MAYOR GOT RE-ELECTED. PEOPLE FELT SAFER. AS LONG AS THE MEDIA KEPT INVENTING BAD GUYS FOR THEM TO FEAR, THEY HAPPILY ACCEPTED THE MARTIAL LAW AND THE MILITARY PRESENCE.
MY CRIME WENT FROM ASSAULTING A POLICE OFFICE TO SOMETHING ELSE, MORE LIKE TREASON. I CHANGE MY NAME. THE TATTOOS HELPED. THE PICTURE MY SCHOOL SUPPLIED THE COPS DIDN'T REALLY LOOK LIK ME AT ALL ANYMORE. I NEVER WENT BACK TO MY APARTMENT.

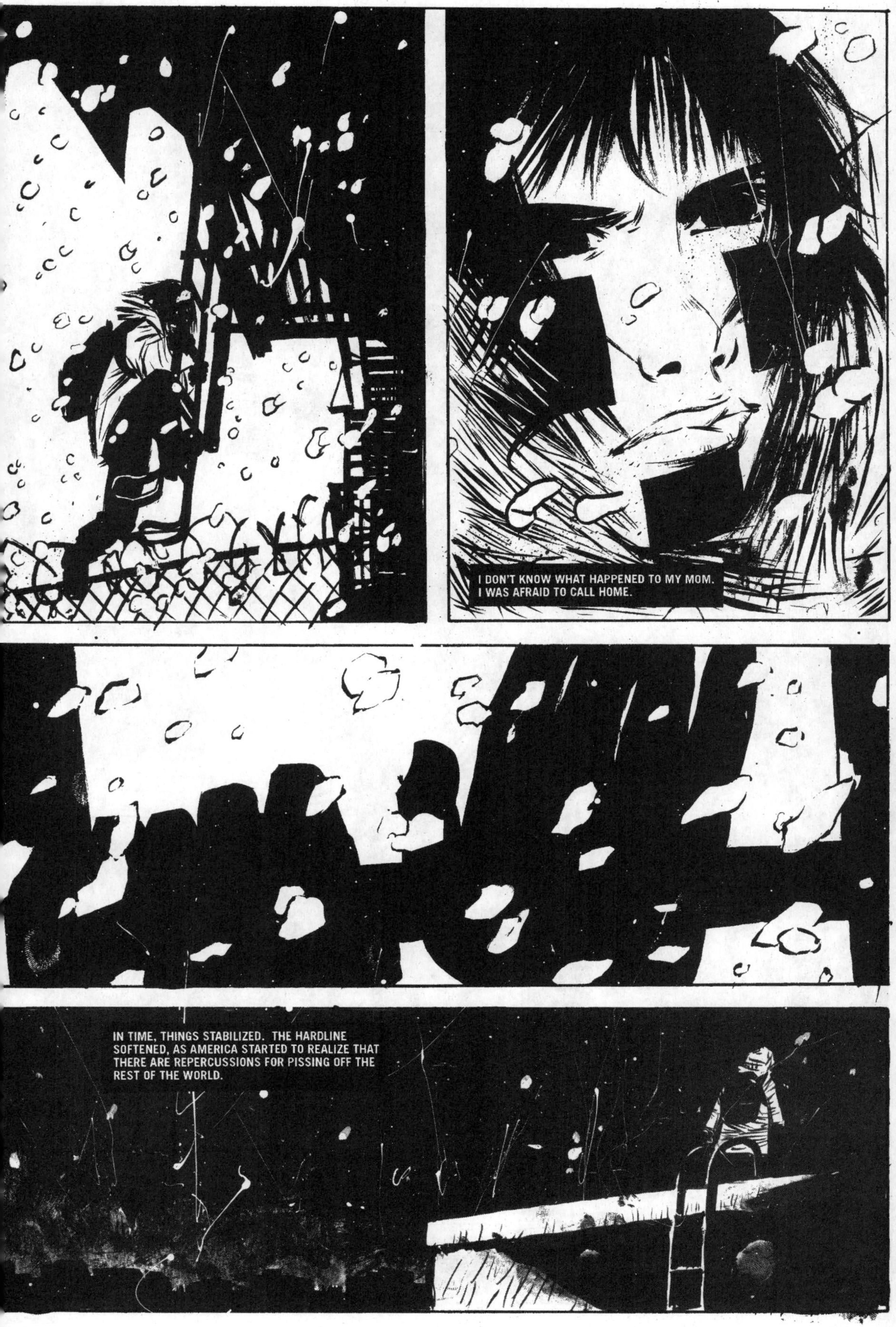
I DON'T KNOW WHAT HAPPENED TO MY MOM.
I WAS AFRAID TO CALL HOME.
IN TIME, THINGS STABILIZED. THE HARDLINE SOFTENED, AS AMERICA STARTED TO REALIZE THAT THERE ARE REPERCUSSIONS FOR PISSING OFF THE REST OF THE WORLD.

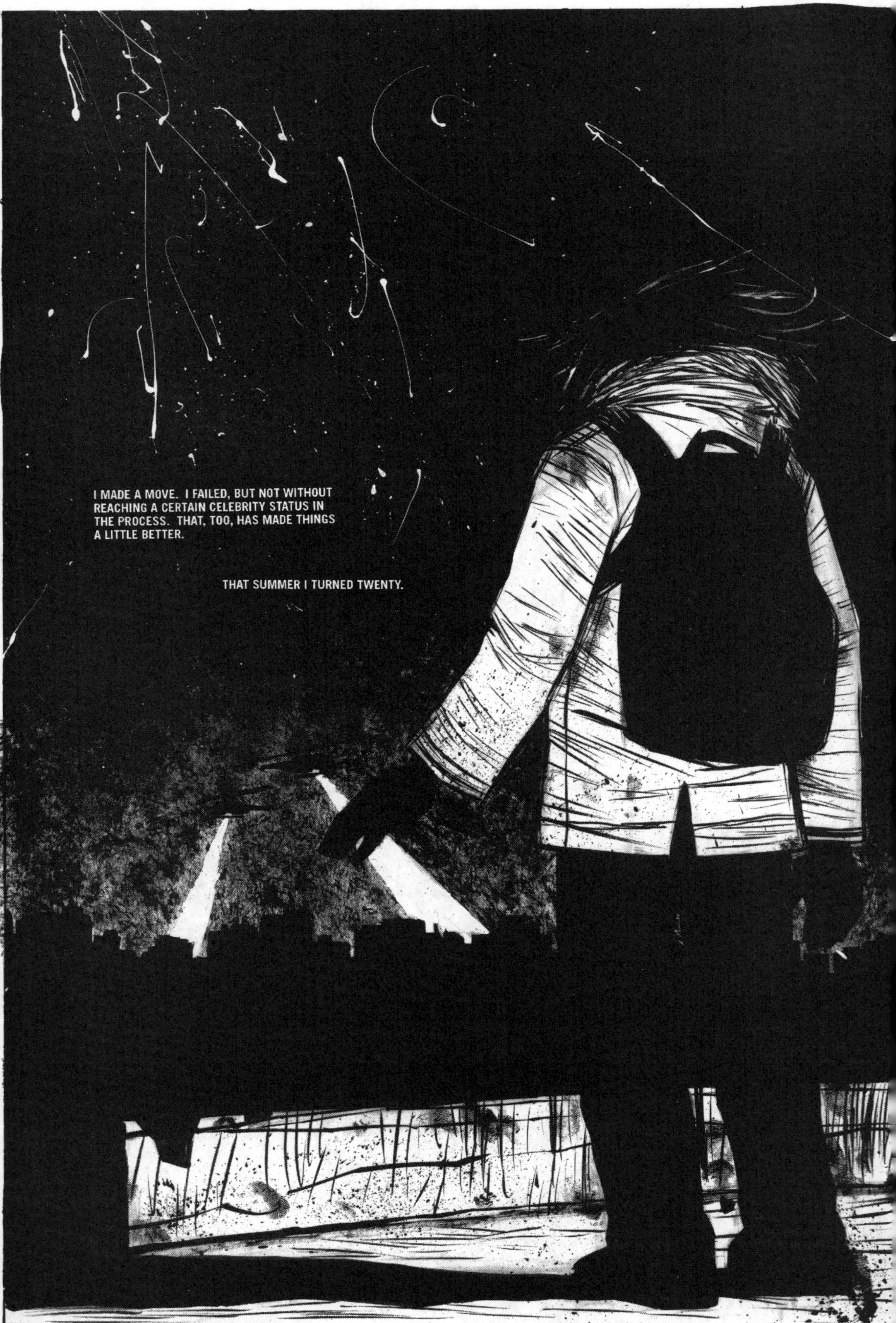
I MADE A MOVE. I FAILED, BUT NOT WITHOUT REACHING A CERTAIN CELEBRITY STATUS IN THE PROCESS. THAT, TOO, HAS MADE THINGS A LITTLE BETTER.
THAT SUMMER I TURNED TWENTY.

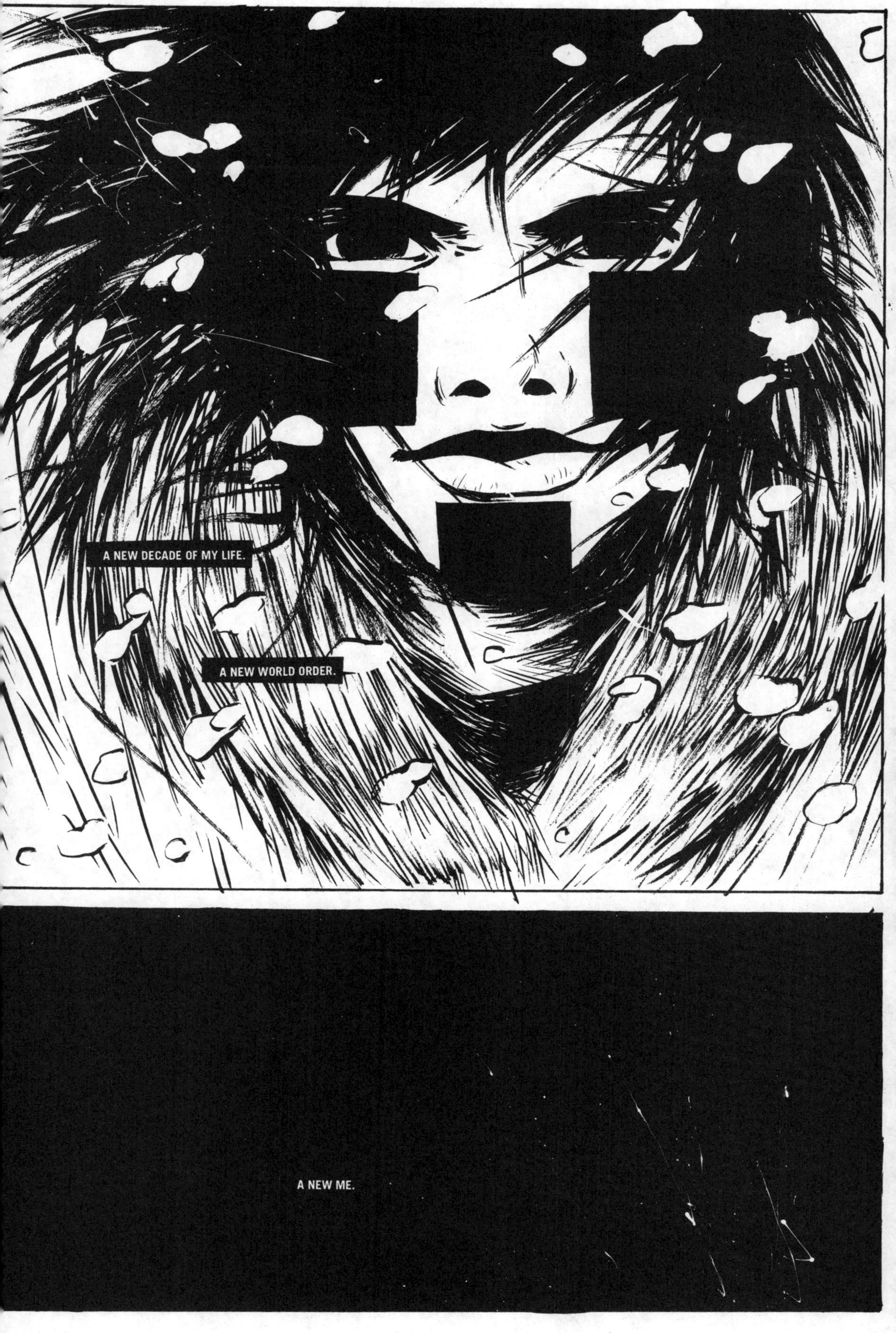
A NEW DECADE OF MY LIFE.
A NEW WORLD ORDER.
A NEW ME.

THE END

(writer) **BRIAN WOOD**
BECKY CLOONAN (artist)

(Photo credit: Jonathan Mukai)

BRIAN WOOD is a writer, artist, designer and producer. He is best known for his graphic novel CHANNEL ZERO, as well as COUSCOUS EXPRESS, PUBLIC DOMAIN, FIGHT FOR TOMORROW, THE COURIERS, and POUNDED, He's contributed to the world of the X-Men with a short writing stint on Marvel Comics' GENERATION X, and is currently a graphic designer on the popular videogame franchises Grand Theft Auto and Midnight Club. Brian lives and works in Brooklyn, New York.

Becky Cloonan draws all the time, self publishing an army of mini comics and zines from her apartment in queens. She is a member of Estrigious Studio, and has work in MeatHaus and other anthologies. Besides comics she has done freelance illustration, and storyboards and animation for the movie Super Troopers (Fox 2001). In her spare time she makes flyers for local shows, and does art for several bands and record lables. Somehow it all seems to work out.